WHEN GROWNUPS PLAY AT WAR

A CHILD'S MEMOIR

by Ilona Flutsztejn-Gruda

TRANSLATED BY
Sarah Cummins

SUMACH PRESS

LIBRARY AND ARCHIVES CANADA CATALOGUING IN PUBLICATION

Flutsztejn-Gruda, Ilona, 1930-
[Quand les grands jouaient à la guerre. English]
When grownups play at war: a child's memoir/Ilona Flutsztejn-Gruda;
translator: Sarah Cummins.

Translation of: Quand les grands jouaient à la guerre.

ISBN 1-894549-43-0

1. Flutsztejn-Gruda, Ilona, 1930- — Childhood and youth.
2. Jewish children in the Holocaust — Poland — Biography. 3. Holocaust,
Jewish (1939-1945) — Poland — Personal narratives.
4. Refugees, Jewish — Poland — Biography.
I. Cummins, Sarah   II. Title.   III. Title: Quand les grands
jouaient à la guerre. English.

PS8611.L88Q3413 2005   940.53'18'092
C2005-900668-4

Originally pubished in French as *Quand les grands jouaient
à la guerre* by Actes Sud Junior
Copyright © 1999 Actes Sud Junior

Edited by Jennifer Day
Designed by Elizabeth Martin
Cover photograph courtesy of Ilona Flutzstejn-Gruda

*Sumach Press acknowledges the support of the Canada Council
for the Arts and the Ontario Arts Council for our publishing program.
We acknowledge the financial support of the Government of Canada through the
Book Publishing Industry Development Program (BPIDP)
for our publishing activities.*

ONTARIO ARTS COUNCIL
CONSEIL DES ARTS DE L'ONTARIO

Printed and bound in Canada

Published by

SUMACH PRESS
1415 Bathurst Street #202
Toronto ON Canada M5R 3H8

*sumachpress@on.aibn.com
www.sumachpress.com*

Introduction

ILONA GRUDA'S STORY of her childhood during the Second World War begins in pre-war Poland. The family, secular Jews who were well assimilated into Polish culture, lived in Miedzeszyn, a village about thirty kilometres east of Warsaw, where both her parents worked. The era between the World Wars was a time of shifting borders in Europe. Poland had long been a territory occupied by a variety of forces, but in 1939, with war looming, Poland was an independent country in military alliance with Britain and France. On September 1, 1939, German troops under Hitler invaded Poland from the north, west and south. Shortly after, on September 17, Soviet forces under Joseph Stalin invaded Poland from the east. Although later in the war the Soviet Union and Germany were to become deadly enemies, from 1939 to 1941 they were allies.

Just before the invasion of Poland on August 23, 1939, Germany and the Soviet Union had signed a secret nonagression pact agreeing to partition Poland between them. By early October, its armed forces defeated, the Polish government surrendered and Poland was occupied, divided into German and Soviet regions. The peaceful childhood that Ilona and her neighbourhood friends had enjoyed was ended.

Ilona was born in 1930; she was only nine when Poland was invaded. By the time she was able to celebrate the end of the Second World War, on May 9, 1945, she was a young woman of fifteen. When she and her family finally returned from exile in Uzbekistan and the Soviet Union, newly liberated Poland was a place transformed by more than five years of foreign occupation. Although Poland was again an independent country, it was soon to come under Soviet control.

That the family had survived at all, despite displacement, starvation and illness, was miraculous, a mixture of good luck and good judgement. Ilona's father had left home to enter the Polish army before its defeat, but instead he ended up resettling and waiting for his family to join him in Wilno (the Polish name for the city of Vilnius). Wilno was then part of Lithuania, which was still at peace. Polish civilians, particularly Jews, had begun to scatter in search of refuge; some fleeing east from the Germans, others moving west to escape the Soviets.

Ilona's own odyssey begins when she and her mother leave their home in Miedzeszyn to join her father, stopping first in the Polish city of Bialystok, and then carrying on to Wilno. There were two dangerous borders to cross: first the one separating the German and Russian occupation zones, and then the border between Russian-occupied Poland and Lithuania.

Although in June of 1940 Lithuania became a Soviet republic, the family remained in Wilno under relatively peaceful conditions. The following year, 1941, on June 22, Germany invaded the Soviet portion of Poland in complete disregard for the nonagression pact between them. The two countries that had happily divided up Poland now abruptly became enemies at war. And within a few days, Lithuania had become part of the battleground. Wilno quickly fell, but the Flutsztejns are able to escape and their migration eastward continues.

As a humanitarian effort, throughout the Soviet Republics the Russians organized mass evacuation of civilians east-ward. Refugees travelled any way they could — walking, begging for rides with the convoys of retreating Russian troops, scrambling for places on the civilian evacuation trains. Some, like the Flutsztejns, stopped in towns along the banks of the Volga, and then, fleeing the harsh winter as well as the encroaching battle front, continued further east by train to the Republics of Uzbekistan and Tajikistan. In the midst of war, they became a mostly harmonious cosmopolitan community of refugees and exiles, Koreans, Ukrainians, Russians, Jews of diverse origin and largely Muslim Uzbeks.

By 1944, the tide of war has begun to turn. The Flutsztejns are anxious to leave the Soviet Union and return to Poland as soon as possible. The first step in their journey back westward is to the Russian capital Moscow, in April of 1945. Once Poland is liberated, the family returns in October 1946 to Lodz in Poland, finally home.

In the story that follows, you will come to see just what it was like to live through such journeys in such times through Ilona's eyes, from the perspective of someone who was really there.

Ilona in 1935

Prologue

IT WAS THE SUMMER OF 1939, the last summer before the Second World War — the war that was to turn the lives of millions of people upside down. I was nine years old. The grownups talked about the approach of war and tried to figure out what they could do to keep safe; I was busy with other things. It was the last peaceful summer vacation, and we children played as we always had, without realizing it was the last time.

We were a group of children between five and twelve years old, all living on the same street in Miedzeszyn, a little village in Poland about thirty kilometres east of Warsaw. My house was at 39 Main Street, the last house before the train station for the little steam engine that ran between Warsaw and Otwock. A new electric train line now linked the two cities, so this station was rarely used. The new station was at the other end of Main Street.

Next to our house was Aunt Mania's house. She took in a few long-term boarders and also rented rooms to vacationers. Lots of children came every summer. The same ones almost always came back, so we knew one another very well.

But first I must tell you about the most important person in my life at that time: my cousin Hala, the daughter of my Aunt Liza, my father's only sister.

The two of us had been born three months apart. Our families lived in the same house and Hala and I slept in the same room. We were also in the same grade at school, although we didn't sit on the same bench and we didn't have the same friends. We were hardly ever apart. We played together all day long, and at night, once the door to our room was closed and the light turned out, we told stories to our hearts' content. In these stories, we were beautiful princesses who had thrilling adventures. I don't remember much about these adventures except that they were always wonderfully exciting and dangerous.

Hala was different from me in many ways. She was much better behaved than I was, and always did what she was told. We often fought because of this, and our parents would also quarrel, as Hala's parents would blame me for whatever trouble we got into. Sure, they were often right, but my feelings were still hurt by their sometimes thoughtless accusations. I must admit that I wasn't always a perfect "sister" to Hala, and no doubt I teased her a bit too much.

One little story shows rather well how different our two personalities were. I still feel ashamed about it. Our school had organized a raffle — I can't remember if it was for Christmas or Easter — and each child won a chocolate animal wrapped in pretty silver paper. I had quite a sweet tooth and as soon as I got home, I devoured my own chocolate bunny. Hala had a chocolate rooster, which stood untouched for a long time on the dresser in our room. Then, little by little, I began to nibble away at the back of the rooster. Nothing showed from the front. By the time Hala found out what I had been up to, I had nibbled an enormous hole in the back. Poor Hala cried bitterly and I felt awful and hateful. Fifty-five years have gone by since then, and I still feel just as bad.

My cousin Inka was also very important in my life. Her mother, "Aunt" Sabina, was a cousin of my father's. Inka was the same age as Hala and I, but she spent the school year in Warsaw and only came to Miedzeszyn for the summer holidays. This made her seem much more interesting than we were — an opinion she clearly shared! She was a bossy girl and it was usually Inka who decided what we would play and who would play what part. I wasn't much of a leader myself, but I didn't like someone else deciding for me. So from time to time, I would stomp off, refusing to play. In our group of children there were also Jurek and Jasia, younger children we all liked to boss around; Hans, Irena, and Gisela, three children of a mixed Jewish and German couple who had been expelled from Germany by Hitler in 1938; and Janusz and Joseph, who also spent their summer vacation in Miedzeszyn. Sometimes children who were only around for a few days also joined us.

I don't remember all the games that kept us busy from morning to evening — only that we were completely absorbed in them. We built tents and pretended we were Indians. We climbed trees, rode our bikes on nearby trails, and played on the swings Aunt Mania had had set up. We made slingshots and bows and arrows for our archery championships, and we built furniture out of old pine branches. And we stubbornly kept open the hole in the fence that separated our yard from Aunt Mania's, despite her endless scoldings. Some games were less innocent, if not very original, such as when the boys showed the girls who could pee the farthest. We girls felt it wasn't fair, but since we were unavoidably handicapped, we had to accept it and watch the contest enviously. Although every parent forbade it, we played the games of "belly to belly" and "tongue to tongue" in secret. I can still recall the bitter taste of someone else's tongue, pleasant and unpleasant at the same time. We had no idea why our parents reacted the way they did.

And so the summer of 1939 unfolded, just like all the summers before. Towards the end of the holidays, however, the spectre of war began to hover over our days. We had to help dig an air raid shelter behind our house. It was deep enough for an adult to sit down inside, and was covered only with boards. There were benches inside so people could spend the twenty or thirty minutes of the drill more comfortably. Then came the drills, terrifying to us children: the shrill sound of the siren, going down into the shelter, the worried voices of the adults discussing whether we would be safe in this hole in the ground during a real air raid.

Later, when the real bombings started, the little hallway in the middle of the house seemed to be a safer spot and that is where the whole family huddled. I am including our dog Puk, who squeezed into the tightest spot in the house, all the while whimpering fearfully.

I haven't yet described our dogs, two other important characters from my childhood. Puk was a Doberman; he had no pedigree even though he looked like a purebred, with his ears and tail docked like a real Doberman. I didn't care about his pedigree. Puk was a good playmate, but he was hostile to strangers. He had to be locked up, to keep him from getting into trouble. Our other dog, Mik, was not allowed inside. Mik looked like a German shepherd but was gentle and good-natured. He spent all his time chained to his doghouse and he loved visits. He was much younger than Puk and showed him great respect, acting like a puppy whenever Puk was around.

I also remember trying on our gas masks. Hala and I had masks specially designed for children, and we always had to practise putting them on so that we could do it quickly. I didn't like this drill, because I couldn't breathe well inside the mask. And I was terrified I wouldn't be able to put it on in time.

Chapter 1

WHO WAS I BACK THEN — what did I feel, what did I like and dislike? I will try to dig out all that is buried in my memory, everything just as it was.

My name is Ilona, but at home I was called by all sorts of nicknames, like Ilonka or Ilusia. I must say right off the bat that I didn't like my name. All the other girls had "normal" first names, like Halina, Zofia, or Janina. Why did I have to be called Ilona, such an unusual name which didn't suit me at all? Then, compared to the other girls, I was rather plump. From my very first year of school, when I was seven years old, the boys called me "Fatty". I would reply with an air of indifference that "when the fat grow thin, the thin will die", but their taunts hurt me. To make it worse, my hair was cut very short — my mother claimed that made it stronger, and she stubbornly refused to understand why I envied the long braids Hala and Inka wore. I thought I was ugly, and this belief was regularly confirmed by the many visitors who exclaimed how lovely Hala and Inka were and totally ignored me.

I was considered lively and intelligent, which was no consolation, especially since I was constantly reproached for being naughty and mischievous. It seems to me that I wasn't such an unruly child. I remember that if my mother forbade me to go barefoot, I didn't disobey outright; I would just go and ask permission from my father, who was much more easygoing.

My parents were both from very poor Jewish families and their childhoods had been much harder than my own. My Papa had lost his mother when he was two and his father when he was fifteen. He was raised by his aunt, and I believe he only went to primary school for four or five years. But he was a gifted and intelligent man; he had taught himself bookkeeping and before the war he worked in a large watch factory. He was also the superintendent of several apartment buildings and earned a very good living. Later in high school and college, when I did my math homework he liked to read the problems and could usually solve them quickly, although he had never studied algebra or geometry. I am sure that he would have gone far if he had stayed in school. He was a friendly, cheerful man, with a great sense of humour. People liked him immensely, especially women. And he liked them, too, as I found out later on.

I learned a lot from Papa, often because he learned things alongside me. Together we learned how to swim, to ride a bicycle, to skate. He hadn't done any of those things when he was a child but he thought they were important, so he did all he could to make sure I could learn them.

He also invited other children and their parents to "social evenings". For these he prepared parlour games, jokes, and magic tricks. I recall eating apples hanging from a string without using our hands, and a prank involving a plate stuck to the ceiling (you had to persuade someone else to hold it up with a broomstick). Nowadays, parents often play with their children, but at the time my father was unusual.

He was proud of me because I was fearless — I would climb trees just like the boys — I was happy and full of energy. The day he found out that I was terrified of going in the water, he showed only encouragement and patience. He went in first and then, with a big smile, held his arms out to me. Slowly, step by step, we went in deeper, holding hands, until my feet could no longer touch bottom. He did this so gently and so gradually that I had no cause to panic. Even today I am afraid of the water, but only if I go in deeper than I went with my father.

How difficult it is for me to speak of my mother. Our relationship was much more complicated. Although she has now been dead for several years, I haven't totally come to terms with it. I loved her greatly but I always had grudges and resentments against her, even since my earliest childhood. I have never managed to get over these feelings.

My mother's family were simple folk. Her father was a shoemaker, with little schooling, although his brothers all had university degrees. He was considered the failure of the family and had broken off nearly all ties with them. My mother hated her father; she told us he was rude to her mother and had nothing to do with his children. His shop did fairly well, but he brought little money home because he lost most of it at cards.

But Mama adored her own mother. She spoke of her as a beautiful, elegant woman who was unhappily married, though I had the impression that her mother was not really interested in her children either. She often left them alone at home all day, with nothing but dry bread to eat. Mama would wait up for her late into the night, hoping that she would bring back something good to eat, and sometimes she did.

From a really young age, my mother was determined to finish her schooling. Her parents thought that only boys needed an education, that her wish was only a little girl's whim. Girls were supposed to marry and have children, and there was no need to attend school for that. Every month, she had the same battle with her mother to get the money for her school fees.

My mother was much more high strung and strict than my father. She worried constantly about my health — I was often sick as a child — and, because of this, forbade many of the things that I enjoyed. She was upset when I climbed trees or did somersaults or rode my bicycle with no hands. If I hurt myself, which I did regularly, or if I tore my clothes or got dirty, she would always look at me with an air of great disappointment. Whenever she got completely exasperated, she would whip me with the leather strop my father used to sharpen his razor. I have forgotten the pain, but not the humiliation and the sense of injustice I felt. She was always bossy and domineering. She told me how I should dress, who my friends should be, what I should study, what I should grow up to be. As a result, I usually did exactly the opposite.

Now I can see better why she acted this way towards her only child and adored daughter, but at the time I couldn't understand her behaviour at all, let alone accept it. Even now, I don't believe in "forgive and forget". For me, even if you manage to forgive, that doesn't mean that you can forget.

Aunt Liza, Hala's mother, was very important to me. My parents both worked in Warsaw and got home late in the evening, when I was already in bed, so I saw very little of them during the week, although of course they were there on Sundays and holidays. Aunt Liza couldn't work because she was very ill. She had trouble walking for more than a quarter of an hour at a time and she was often tired. Once a day the door to her bedroom was closed while someone changed her "dressing". We weren't allowed in the room at those times, not even near the door. No one told us what the "dressing" was, and the air of mystery made it even more disturbing.

Most of the time Aunt Liza sat in her armchair, reading or knitting. We had two servants: a governess, who looked after the children, and a housekeeper, who did the housework and cooked our meals. Our governess also looked after Aunt Liza. Aunt Liza always played with us and I loved her because she was so gentle and calm, despite her illness. She taught us to sew, crochet, and knit, so we could make clothes for our dolls, and she showed us how to make doll dishes out of the silver wrappers from chocolate bars. She also wrote plays for us to perform. Aunt Liza was in charge of directing, sets, and casting, while Hala, Inka, a few neighbourhood children and I were the actors. I remember once I played the role of the moon in one of these plays. I was upset about this, because Hala and Inka had bigger parts and, more annoyingly, much nicer costumes. My costume was a dark blue sheet that was supposed to be the sky, with a large yellow circle on it. I had to stay in the background, balanced on a stack of benches and chairs. Of course, it all collapsed with a tremendous crash during the dress rehearsal. Luckily, no one was hurt. On opening night, Aunt Zosia (my mother's sister, who would visit us from time to time before the war) stood behind me to make sure I didn't fall.

Uncle Yona, Aunt Liza's husband, was the real terror of my childhood. He was even stricter than my mother. Whenever we started to play some exciting game, he would loom up, tall and threatening, demanding to know what we were playing. Usually, he forbade it. He wouldn't even let us leave a bit earlier in the morning to play with the other children in the schoolyard, and Hala was not allowed to read any books that he considered stupid. He mostly picked on Hala, but I remember I hated him with a passion. It was only much later, when we were together again after the war, that I came to know and love this man.

My family and Hala's shared a single house. It was just a small house, with three bedrooms, a room where we ate our meals, and a large kitchen, with a small room next to it for the servants. In the past, our parents' families had lived in cities for generations, crowded into dark apartments looking out over narrow, steep courtyards. They had never owned a house, let alone a country home. But my father had always dreamed of living in the country, being in touch with nature, tending a garden. I don't know how he came up with the money to buy land, or what made him decide to build a house for us to share with his beloved only sister and her family.*

Our house was surrounded by a pretty garden, full of flowers and shrubbery. There was a lawn crossed by two lanes, one bordered by roses and one by lilacs. We could run or ride our bikes along these lanes, and in the winter we flooded the larger one to turn it into a skating rink.

We weren't allowed to go beyond the boundaries of the garden, but we were intrigued by the little wood behind the house. Village rumour had it that strange and frightful things happened in that wood. In one tale, a man who was walking from Otwock to Warsaw dropped dead there from exhaustion. Another story told of a woman giving birth to six puppies in the wood. All of this caught our imaginations, and for a long time I saw the little wood as a magical place of enchantment.

When I returned to Miedzeszyn several years later, I found only a few spindly trees and no trace of magic. The mountain across from our house that we had sledded and skied down was nothing but a little hill.

But I still remember that house and everything around it as perfection, and I look back on that part of my childhood with great nostalgia.

It was my only real childhood. The war left its terrible mark on everything that came after.

* Papa and his sister Liza had lost their mother at an early age — Aunt Liza was four and Papa only two — and they had been separated for a long time when Aunt Liza was sent to their maternal grandmother and Papa to their paternal aunt. The two families didn't get along and the children hardly ever saw each other. Despite or perhaps because of this, Papa and Liza were so close as adults that they chose to live together, and so we shared the house in Miedzeszyn.

Chapter 2

IT HAPPENED on a beautiful September day, a real Polish September day with a splendid blue sky. From this clear sky the planes began to drop bombs.

The planes were bombing Warsaw. In Miedzeszyn we heard the explosions and saw the squadrons flying past, more and more of them. When the radio announced that war had broken out, Aunt Sabina frantically herded all us children together and started running with us away from the planes, away from the bombs. We were overcome by panic. Even though nothing had happened to us, we were terrified at the thought of what might happen any moment.

Aunt Liza stopped our senseless flight. She calmed Sabina down and took us back home for a glass of lemonade. We were reassured by her calm and serenity.

But the war that people had been talking about for months was upon us. I don't remember the first days very well. Whenever we heard the rumble of the planes and the sound of distant explosions, we rushed to the hallway in the middle of the house to try to keep safe from bombs and shrapnel. I was very frightened, even though I didn't really know what was going on. Puk huddled in his corner, whimpering pitifully.

The grocery store was closed, and there was nowhere

to buy food. Fortunately, we had some supplies in the cellar — a few sacks of flour, some jars of jam, and some canned food. Hala and I were delighted: no more spinach or carrots, no more horrible-tasting dishes that were supposed to be good for you. Home-made white bread spread with jam suited us just fine. We secretly shared our snacks with Puk, who otherwise had to make do with barley porridge. Aunt Sabina and Inka left, as did all our holiday friends and our two servants. It was sad to say goodbye to Regina, our governess. Happily, Aunt Zosia came to take the servants' place. My mother had complained of being lonely, and the two sisters were very fond of one another. We liked Aunt Zosia too, since we could play all sorts of tricks on her and she never scolded us. She was very patient and understanding.

The war seemed to be happening somewhere else far away. People were fighting and being killed, but it didn't really affect us.

All this changed completely on September 6th or 7th, when all men of combat age were ordered by radio to the eastern part of the country, where new divisions would be formed to halt the enemy invasion. My father, who was forty-three years old, and Uncle Yona, who was fifty, immediately packed their knapsacks, picked up their gas masks, and set off to defend their country. We said our farewells on the hill near the railway station. Papa, Mama and I sat on the ground, disconsolate; Hala and her parents were a little way off. I don't remember what we talked about; I only recall our sadness and anxiety. Would we ever see one another again?

Scenes of men saying goodbye to their families as they set off to war are as old as the human race. But for me, it was the first time, and the man who was leaving was my beloved Papa. I promised him that I would keep a diary that he could read on his return, which I did conscientiously for a few weeks. I remember that I wrote letters and a few poems in the diary. I thought the poems were rather good, but after the grownups made fun of my efforts, I gave up writing them. Unfortunately this diary has been lost.

The train arrived and "our men" boarded. With heavy hearts, we tearfully returned to the house. And life went on, the harsh existence of wartime.

Now all the responsibility fell on my mother's shoulders. She was the most energetic and ended up in charge of everything. This wasn't the first time she had been in such a situation. During the First World War she had had to run the household, even though she was hardly more than a child. Her father was dying and her brothers and sisters were dazed and disoriented. She had always been the strongest, the most responsible, so it fell to her to make the important decisions. Her choices often seemed arbitrary and sometimes unfair, and some of them led to tragedy, but in those troubled times it was hard to know what to do. At the time I often felt extremely resentful of my mother. It was only much later that I understood how hard it must have been for her.

After my father and my uncle left, my mother began to prepare for winter. With other women from the neighbourhood, she made frequent trips into the countryside to buy potatoes and other supplies. She even managed to find some coal.

She also rode her bicycle into Warsaw to collect some salary she was owed. Her boss had no money to pay his employees, so instead he handed out boxes of wax and polish produced by his factory. These were of no use to us. Clean, well-polished floors and shoes were the least of our concerns! When she got back home, Mama told us that the German bombs had damaged much of the city. People had been killed and many had been injured, but fortunately all of our family and friends were safe and sound.

Our house became a hub of activity. People would come, spend a few days, and then leave for who knows where. I had a feeling that some plan was being hatched, but I had no idea what it was. There was restlessness and anxiety in the air.

Hala and I often played with Kristina, who lived in the fourth house on our street. It was a big house in a yard with very old trees. I remember one of these trees in particular. It had great branches where each of us had her own "apartment"; there we would host afternoon tea and hold dinner parties. School was closed, so we could play all day long. Nobody kept tabs on us, so we had much more freedom than before.

The Germans had already reached Warsaw. Soon the first of their patrols appeared in Miedzeszyn. Several came and searched our house, looking for the men. The soldiers held up men's clothing to prove that there must be men there. It was always Aunt Zosia who dealt with them, since she spoke German very well and she didn't look Jewish. This was to become important, later on in the occupation.

Aunt Zosia was a pretty woman, elegant and distinguished. She inspired respect in the German soldiers, who were still behaving decently with the Polish population in general and Jews in particular. But their attitude changed very soon.

One heartbreaking event stands out in my memory of that time. Mama decided we could no longer feed two large dogs, and naturally her verdict fell on poor dumb Mik. She asked two German soldiers who were passing through to kill him, which they were happy to do. Hala and I were both stricken, and I found it hard to forgive my mother. We buried poor Mik at the back of the garden. This was the first funeral in my life.

The first war news from Papa and Uncle Yona was of the hazards they faced as they made their way eastward. Of course, no army had been formed; everything was in chaos. The roads were overflowing with people on foot wandering in all directions. Government and institutional officials were fleeing Poland by car across the Romanian border. The Russian invasion of Poland in the east, commonly known as "the knife in the back", caused even greater panic and chaos.

It was very hard for all these people to get food and even drinking water. Uncle Yona was so exhausted and discouraged that at one point he simply lay down on the ground and refused to go further. Fortunately, he was persuaded to continue.

Finally, he and Papa arrived at Wilno, held at the time by Lithuania. Papa and Uncle Yona were doing well there; they had found work and a large apartment. Yona had a rich brother in Riga, the capital of neighbouring Latvia, and he was helping Papa and Uncle Yona out financially. They felt secure and figured that Wilno was a perfect spot to wait out the war, so they decided to send for us. This proved to be a very wise decision. At the time it was fairly easy to cross borders. Some people, mostly Jews, were fleeing the Germans, while others were running from the Soviets, who had already begun to deport Poles to Siberia. But in Wilno, all was calm and life was good. Shops were well-stocked, adults had work, children could attend school. One could almost forget there was a war going on. But no one could predict what the future would hold.

There was no question of two women and two children making such a trek alone, so it was arranged that two guides would come soon to fetch us.

While we waited, we prepared for our journey. The two guides didn't show up when expected, and Mama bicycled into Warsaw nearly every day to get news. We were anxious and worried about all the contradictory rumours. Every evening Mama reported what she had learned in town, and none of it was good news. We heard that the Germans were stopping people at the border and putting them in prison, that disreputable guides would abandon their charges at night in the forest. Those abandoned were left to wander for hours until they fell into the hands of border guards. The Russians sent the fugitives to the Germans,* and the Germans threw them in prison.

I listened fearfully to all these conversations. I absorbed the stories like a sponge, and grew more and more afraid.

I also listened to the emotional discussions about who would come with us. Of course my mother, Aunt Liza, Hala and I would be part of the group, but we did not know how Aunt Liza, so sickly and delicate, could manage such a trying journey. Aunt Zosia, who suffered from tuberculosis, also wished to come. My mother insisted that the journey would be impossible with two children and two invalids and tried to convince her sister to stay in our comfortable, well-stocked house and wait for us to come back at the end of the war.

If only we could have known what turn the war would take. But my mother's brother, Uncle Simon, Ala and Bronek's father, tapped his forehead and said that you'd have to be crazy to abandon such a nice house to set off into the unknown with two children and a sick woman. Uncle Simon and all of his family, who chose to remain, died later at Treblinka, or perhaps in the Warsaw ghetto. Later, someone told my mother that he had seen Ala, with only a newspaper to cover her, dying in the street. We learned of Aunt Zosia's death toward the end of the war from the owner of a house where she had rented a room. We had nearly made it to her while she was still alive. Apparently, Zosia blamed my mother. Mama felt a terrible guilt all her life, and often wept when she spoke of

* who were still allies at that time

her. At the time, I was very angry that Mama had refused to bring Aunt Zosia along. And even today, I remember her with great sadness. I can still picture her standing on the steps of our house saying goodbye to us. She stood tall and upright, her blonde hair pulled back in a bun, waving a handkerchief as she tried to hold back her tears. Could she have felt a premonition of the fate that awaited her?

But no one could have imagined the nightmare that was soon to begin. No one could have believed that the Germans, considered by the entire world to be civilized and cultured, would coldly and systemically exterminate another people.

Mama and Aunt Liza were undertaking this difficult, dangerous journey because Uncle Yona and Papa wanted us to be with them and thought that Wilno was a good place to wait out the war. How could they know that those who stayed behind were condemned to die?

Our guides finally came. They were railway workers who knew the lay of the land on both sides of the border. They told us that everything was set. They had chosen the place where we would wait before crossing the border and arranged for a person to help us cross on the first night that was dark enough. There were actually two frontiers to cross: one separating the German and Russian occupation zones, near Malkinia, the town we were to reach by train; and then the border between Russia and Lithuania.

Mama had packed our bags, big sacks filled with whatever she thought would be needed in our new life.

But the guides said we could not take them, since we had a long way to go on foot at night, and we would never be able to carry it all. In the end, we only took what was needed for the few days of the trip.

And so we left. First we took the train to Warsaw, where we found out that not all Germans were as polite and civilized as those we had known in Miedzeszyn. The station was packed. We heard piercing shrieks, dogs barking, even gunshots. I had no idea what was happening, but I remember how I felt seized by paralyzing fear.

We went to Uncle Simon's house in Warsaw, where we heard nothing but comments on how stupid Mama was to be making this journey.

"Leave such a fine house and such a lovely garden, to sneak across the border with two children and a sick woman! Risk prison and God knows what else! You must be out of your mind! You've got to be crazy to do such a thing!" That was what Simon said. He could have no idea of the fate his family would meet after deciding to stay. Mama would not be swayed. Her husband had decided we should come and he had sent the guides. There was no arguing with the decision.

Chapter 3

THE NEXT DAY we started on the second leg of our journey, on the train to the border at Malkinia. We had been told of the terrible things that had happened to others as they stepped off the train: Germans, dogs, gunshots ... But luck was with us: the train stopped at the semaphore signal before the station. The guides ordered us to jump off with them immediately, and they lifted Aunt Liza down in their arms. The train left, and we were spared the danger of running into Germans at the station.

We were in a huge field, completely empty except for a few trees here and there. It was freezing cold, as it was December and that winter was an exceptionally bad one. The guides decided to go into the village to find the man whose house we were to stay at before crossing the border. They told us to wait for them beside the trees.

I had heard so many stories about crooked guides who took people's money and then abandoned them that I was terribly afraid that they would never return. Even though we knew the name of the farmer who was supposed to take us in, we had no idea how to get to his house. We were very cold. Night had fallen and we were in total darkness. Aunt Liza could hardly stand. Weak with exhaustion, she leaned shakily against a tree trunk. Far away we could hear gunshots and dogs barking.

I don't know how much time passed, but it seemed like an eternity.

Finally our guides came back. They told us that it was lucky we had waited there, because in the village the Germans had caught and arrested other people who were fleeing. The Germans had gone now, and it was safe to head for our shelter. It was quite a long walk, and we had to go slowly because of Aunt Liza. Finally we arrived at the farmer's house, a fairly large thatched cottage with two bedrooms and a huge kitchen heated by an enormous woodstove. We were to sleep behind it; several people were already doing just that. They squeezed us in, I'm not sure how. A bed was found for Aunt Liza in one of the bedrooms. There was no question of crossing the border that night, and we didn't know if it would be possible the following night either. For the time being, I was very happy that we had a roof over our heads, we were warm, and things were quiet.

The next day was very bright and sunny. Hala and I spent the day in the cottage playing with our hosts' children on a haystack, while our mothers planned what they would say if Germans came to the house asking who we were. They told us to loosen our hair a bit and dirty our faces, so we would look like the other children. They put scarves on our heads to cover our hair, which was much darker than that of the other children. If there was an unexpected visitor, we were to say that we were the neighbours' children. It was harder for my mother and Aunt Liza: they could not be mistaken for peasant women, even if they wore headscarves. But in the end, our fears were for nothing because no one came.

The greatest difficulty that day was when it came time to change Aunt Liza's "dressing". Everyone was sent out of the bedroom and my mother locked herself in with Aunt Liza for what seemed like ages. When she finally came out, she was carrying a package wrapped in newspaper which she threw into the toilet. Only much later did I learn the nature of the mysterious "dressing": Aunt Liza had ulcers of the colon, which made it impossible for her to pass stools in the normal way. She had been fitted with a pouch which had to be emptied and cleaned every day. It was not pleasant, especially in a house full of strangers, with no running water.

The following night it was too clear. The moon was waning, but the stars in the cloudless sky were enough to light the border. We needed darkness to hide our crossing, so we had to spend another day at the cottage. The second evening, as the sky gradually clouded over, we knew the crucial time had come. We set out around ten o'clock, with our guides and the farmer.

After we had been walking for some time through the woods I was so nervous and tense that I began to feel severe cramps. The whole group had to stop while I crouched, embarrassed, in the brush. The guides were impatient and snapped at me to hurry up. They were anxious because it was nearly time for the changing of the border guards, and that would be the best moment to cross. We came out of the woods into a large clearing. The farmer stopped there and told us that once we crossed the clearing we would be safe. He wouldn't go any further with us, which upset everything at the last minute. Our guides argued that he was supposed to take us and we would refuse to pay him until we had crossed the border. Finally everything was worked out and we set off again. We were very frightened as we crossed the clearing. Aunt Liza could hardly walk. After a few steps she stopped and said that she couldn't go on. We helped her to sit down and waited nervously until she felt strong enough again. This probably wasn't for very long, but it seemed like forever. I was expecting the Germans to appear at any moment. Finally the guides lifted her up and, supporting her with their arms, practically carried her so that we could cross the border before the new sentries began their rounds.

We finally came to a little group of shacks on the other side of the clearing. We sat down on the snow next to one of the shacks, while our guides set off to find a place for us to spend the night. We were now in Soviet territory, but the danger was not yet behind us. We remembered the stories of Russians capturing fugitives and delivering them to the Germans. But by good fortune, neither Russians nor Germans were working overtime that night; probably the bitter cold had convinced them to stay inside their snug cabins. The four of us were very cold and exhausted. Hala and I drowsed off and our mothers had to keep shaking us awake and explaining — in whispers, so as not to awaken the inhabitants of the shack — that if we fell asleep in such intense cold, we might never wake up again. Finally, our guides reappeared and took us to another farmer's cottage to spend the night.

This cottage was much smaller, dirtier and more crowded than the first. There were people sleeping everywhere, on benches, at the stove and even on the ground. Hala and I managed to squeeze in around the stove, and Mama and Aunt Liza spent the night sitting on stools. Aunt Liza wound up lying on the floor, since she was so tired, but my mother would rather have died than lie down on that dirty earthen floor.

Very early the next morning, before sunrise, people began to stir around us. We were hurried to a cart waiting outside for us. Once again disguised as peasants with scarves on our heads, we set off. We rode for a long time. It was well into the day when suddenly we saw Papa waiting for us at the side of the road. What relief! What a reunion! All my fears immediately disappeared. Nothing bad could happen to us now, because Papa was with us. He laughed heartily when he saw how we were got up, and reassured us that the border was now far behind us.

We went to the home of one of Mama's uncles, in Bialystok. Again, the same neverending discussions began. Escape the Germans or the Russians? Which were more of a threat to Jews? Mama's uncle was of the opinion that the Germans, who were known to be a highly civilized people, were not as dangerous as the "savage" Russians, who had already started to attack the bourgeoisie. In any case, everyone was sure the war wouldn't last long, because the French and the English were on our side. How could the Germans hold out for long against so many? No one seemed to understand that the drive to fight could make a huge difference. And at that time, only the Germans had that drive.

After a few days and nights in Bialystok, we set off for Wilno, our final destination. I remember little about that last leg of the journey.

Before leaving, my parents hid two watches inside my mittens and told me not to tell anyone about them under any circumstances. Hala received the same instructions. If anyone asked us, "Do you have anything, girls?" we were to raise our hands and answer, "No, nothing." We were put to the test; twice, Lithuanian guards stopped us at the border. They took everything our parents had, but the watches were safe because we did as we were told. The Lithuanian soldiers were very rude. They shouted and insulted us, calling us dirty Jews.

Chapter 4

AT LAST WE HAD reached Lithuania. Another village, another cart ride, and then we were in Wilno. Uncle Yona awaited us in a quiet, warm apartment with a balcony overlooking the street. Danger was behind us now. Hala and I shared a bedroom again; I remember it had wallpaper with all kinds of bizarre little figures. How happy we were, after so many adventures! The danger, the fear, the nights spent in cottages with strange people; it was all over. Nothing bad could happen to us now. We turned back into two little girls concerned only with games and playmates.

It was Christmas time. There was a Christmas tree, and presents and friends who came to visit. Everyone marvelled at Aunt Liza's courage, how she had accomplished such a feat, despite being sick and weak. My mother's role was ignored and she stayed out of the limelight. But I knew she was the real heroine.

After the Christmas holidays, everyday life started up again. It was time to go back to school and our parents decided to enroll us in a Jewish school. Wilno was known for the strong presence of its vibrant Jewish culture, a secular culture expressed in Yiddish. Our parents had never agreed with religious education but they were proud of their Jewishness. They thought it was time that their children learned about the Jewish people and their history.

Up until then, we had been raised in complete ignorance of differences in religions and nationality — quite an unusual upbringing for the time. Our parents believed deeply that people's worth did not depend on their background or religion. The important thing was to be honest, to harm no one, to look out for other people. The rest didn't matter much. Unfortunately, these fine principles were rare at the time.

In Miedzeszyn, we had known nothing about Jews or Poles or God or prayers or anything like that. But in reality, these things did affect the way people treated one another, even children. Our ignorance led us into some situations that seem ironic now. I remember one scene in particular. I was four or five years old and I was playing with some friends on a little hill in front of our house. Suddenly, one of the other children yelled, "The Jews are coming! Let's get out of here!"

He pointed at some strange bearded men, dressed all in black. We all ran off in a panic, shouting and stumbling.

When I started primary school at the age of seven, I still had no idea what religion was all about. On the first day of school, in Grade 2 (Hala and I had skipped Grade 1, because we already knew how to read and write), we were astonished to see the other children kneel down and recite some words, making mysterious gestures with their hands. We hadn't a clue what was going on. We thought this was something the children had learned in Grade 1, so we just imitated them as best we could. There were some Jewish children who remained quietly standing throughout the prayer, but we did not notice them. After class a little girl came up to me.

"Aren't you Jewish?" she asked.

"Yes," I answered. "Why do you ask?" I had a vague impression that I was indeed Jewish, without really knowing what that meant.

"Then why were you praying with the others?"

I had no answer. I shrugged my shoulders and walked away. That was the way it was. We were in total ignorance of a matter that was central in the lives of other children.

Not long after, something else happened, this time more serious. One day after class, a bunch of my schoolmates were chasing another child who was wearing a long black coat and a skullcap. They were shouting "dirty Jew" and throwing stones at him. I joined this exciting game, yelling and throwing stones with the others. This was just the kind of game I liked, with lots of action and fighting. Once I had even organized a battle between the boys and the girls. I didn't understand why this was happening to poor David Goldberg, who was dressed so strangely and ran so awkwardly. He was different from us; of course we persecuted him. Calling him "dirty Jew" meant nothing at all to me; it was just an insult like any other.

Since then, I have often thought about these things. I think this is how racism first began: attacking people who are different brings together the members of a group by giving them a feeling of safety and belonging. We also tormented a red-headed boy in our class, chanting a verse that we had made up: "Redhead in the shed, the shed it fell, hear redhead yell!" The same kind of thing happened between boys and girls: the boys pulled the girls' hair and hit them. Any difference was a good enough reason to make fun of others and hurt them. Since my father had always taught me to stand up for myself, to hit before I got hit, I was naturally one of the attackers and not one of the victims. Hala, however, was a "real" girl and did not get mixed up in these violent games.

The David Goldberg story ended badly for me. One of the boys in the class went and told my father that I had thrown stones at David and yelled "dirty Jew" at him. Papa probably explained things to me at the time, but I have forgotten what he said. I only recall that he ordered me to apologize to David and to give him a chocolate bar. There was no way I was going to apologize to a boy, so I just slipped the chocolate bar into the pocket of his coat hanging in the cloakroom. Knowing my sweet tooth, Papa only asked whether I had given David the chocolate bar. I said with an almost-clear conscience that I had — I wasn't 100 percent certain that the coat belonged to David.

I tell of these things now only to show how astonishing our parents' decision was to enroll us in a Jewish school. Hala and I were mystified, but no one asked us our opinion. Of course, we didn't know a single word of Yiddish. Our parents would sometimes speak Yiddish when they didn't want us to understand what they were saying, but we weren't curious and we never even tried to figure it out. A Yiddish tutor was hired and we had a few months of private lessons at home. In the meantime, whenever a teacher called on us at school, we would politely stand up and say, "We're very sorry, but we don't speak Yiddish." It must have been funny to the other students. This didn't last long: after a few months, we knew enough Yiddish to follow the classes at school.

A lot of things had changed in our life. We quickly made new friends and, as usual, my best friend was not the same as Hala's, although we still played together. We now lived in a big city, and our parents decided that we were no longer little girls and allowed us to go out on our own. We felt very grown up and responsible.

The daily walk from home to school was fairly long and full of surprises. I remember one strange man who would often lurk around the school. When he met our group of girls, he would open his coat and show us his private parts. We would run off in gales of laughter.

I also remember that, for a while, we would find an old three-kopeck coin every day in the same spot. Each time, just the one coin; we imagined that a Prince Charming left them there in hopes of getting to meet us. The coins stopped one day and we never did meet Prince Charming, but we did begin to collect coins . . .

In June of 1940, Lithuania lost its independence and became a Soviet republic. The two other Baltic states, Latvia and Estonia, met the same fate. This hardly affected us at all, though. At school, a course in Russian was added. We learned the Cyrillic alphabet, which I was happy for later. We were forbidden to use the capitalist terms *pan* and *pani* (Mr. and Mrs., or sir and madam). Instead, we were supposed to call everyone *tovarishch*, which meant "comrade". I knew that people were being arrested and sent to Siberia and others were hiding in the villages, but we were told that nothing would happen to us since we were not rich or important. I wasn't much interested in such things. I had my own life, school and friends and play, and that was all that mattered to me.

From our point of view as children, the next year passed with few important events. Hala and I started playing with dolls again. (We had given it up earlier, since we were big girls of ten.) One of our new friends had a huge collection of dolls, with lots of clothes. We were inspired to start a doll collection too, after our stamp and coin collections. We would trade dolls' clothes and accessories with our friend. In the winter, we often went skating. I have a long scar on my right thigh, a souvenir of a skating accident.

In my memory, the summer holiday of 1940 was a very happy one. We spent the whole summer in the countryside, at Pospieszki, not far from Wilno. A gang of boys had a war game going there, and after much pestering, we got them to let us join in. We made rifles, revolvers and other weapons out of wood and bark. The rules were very strict. There wasn't much killing; instead we took prisoners. One day the boys held us prisoner in a sandpit until nightfall. Our families had sent out search parties and were about to call the police when a neighbour found us. We were scolded severely and forbidden to play with the boys for a time, but it soon blew over.

School started up again in the usual way. Nothing special happened until something occurred which affected the rest of my life. At the time it upset me deeply.

Hala and I were like twin sisters. Of course, we argued occasionally, but we couldn't imagine living without each other. Or at least, I couldn't imagine living without her. Even though we had such different personalities, we always played together, walked to school together; we shared many memories and secrets.

Then all of a sudden we found out that we were to be separated. I suppose our parents had been discussing this at home for some time, but it was a complete surprise to us. They only told us once the decision was already final. Hala and her parents were leaving for the United States, while my family would stay in Wilno.

This was in the spring of 1941, just a few months before war was declared between Germany and Russia. Of course, no one knew that far in advance that this was going to happen, but why did my parents not make the same wise choice as my aunt and uncle? I recall very clearly that my father told everyone that war between Russia and Germany was certain and we must prepare for it. He said that we would have to flee the Germans; we should buy bicycles and pack our bags, so we would be ready to leave quickly. I remember several of his friends teasing him, saying that with such a vivid imagination he would do better to write novels. These discussions were lively, and I had the impression that people thought my father was a bit of a fool who was always boring people with the same old story. So why, then, did we not leave for America? It would have been a way to avoid the war. Especially since my father didn't want to be separated from his only sister whom he loved so much.

Mama really didn't want to leave, for two quite different reasons. First, she was a great believer in socialism and didn't wish to leave the Soviet Union, the only country where communists were in power. For her, the Soviet Union was a paradise of justice and equality. No one could convince her otherwise, although most of our friends believed the opposite. Before the war, my mother had been what was called a "Communist sympathizer"; she was not a party member, but she spent time with party comrades and helped them in various ways. Against the wishes of my father and Hala's parents, she allowed militants sought by the police to hide in our house for several days, sometimes even several weeks. She also took packages to others who were in prison.

The other reason was that my mother was fed up with sharing her home with another family. Anyone can understand this. In fact I am surprised that we lived together for as long as we did, especially since Mama and Uncle Yona argued so often. There was even a fairly long time when they didn't speak to one another.

At the time I knew nothing of her reasons, and wouldn't have cared to know. The only thing that mattered was being separated from Hala. A farewell party was organized at school and she was given an album with photos of our classmates. The children and teachers all signed their names. I was very unhappy, but no one seemed to realize how deep my grief was. The most hurtful part was that Hala didn't seem to care; she remained calm and appeared indifferent. Unlike myself, she believed in accepting her fate without protest.

I have no memory of the day they left or of saying goodbye at the railway station. I only recall the enormous emptiness I felt afterwards. Now I was all alone and I would have to get used to it. At the time I believed that it would just be for a while, and that we would be together again after the war. I even made a drawing, on which I wrote America, Warsaw and Wilno at the corners, with Miedzeszyn in the middle. Hala, Inka and I would come running from the three corners of the earth to the promised land of our childhood. This was never to happen, even though all three of us did, fortunately, survive the war. I didn't see Hala again until 1966, after we had been separated for twenty-five years.

So I was alone, deprived of my constant companion. There was no one to play with or to squabble with. I was very, very sad. My life was turned upside down, nothing would ever be the same again. Something essential had been torn from me.

Chapter 5

Now a period of great anxiety set in. There was much coming and going and talk of the threat of war between Germany and the Soviet Union.

Should we try to flee from the Germans? If so, how? Weren't the Russians just as dangerous? The news from Warsaw got worse and worse. Every day the Germans became more cruel. They were keeping Jews confined to a ghetto in appalling conditions: several families crowded together in each unheated apartment, with little to eat. Disease was spreading.

Sending packages to relatives and friends in Warsaw became an important part of our life. Since we could only send small amounts, Mama made sure that everything was high in calories. For example, she would prepare a paste of melted butter, sugar, and cocoa. I remember this because I liked to lick the pot, even though I was neither starving nor wasting away. In fact, I was still rather plump.

On June 22, 1941, bombs fell from a blue sky. This time, they came from right over our heads, not thirty kilometres away as they had in September 1939. People took shelter in cellars, some weeping, others praying loudly. Mingled with these sounds was the roar of the planes and from time to time, a loud explosion told us that a bomb had fallen near our house. I was terrified. My parents tried to calm me as best they could, but their efforts didn't help. I was so frightened that I was oblivious to their words; I didn't even hear them. I was certain that our end was near.

In the lulls between bombings, friends would stop by at the house carrying knapsacks. They were heading east. They said it was time to get out, that the Germans would be there in a couple of days. My parents considered what to do.

"Remember, if we leave, we will have no shelter, we'll have nothing," said my father. "And we'll be leaving behind a comfortable house, like in Miedzeszyn."

I couldn't understand my parents! We had heard so many terrible things about the Germans, and they were still unsure about whether to flee from these monsters! I began to cry, saying over and over, "I'm afraid of the Germans. We have to leave, please, I beg you."

Apparently my cry of distress tipped the balance. A Russian proverb says *Ustami ditati glagolet istina:* the truth comes out of the mouths of babes. That is what my parents must have thought. That very evening, they decided we would leave the next morning. We began to pack. It wasn't easy to decide what to bring. Each item had to be indispensable yet light enough to be carried on our backs. My parents must not have been thinking clearly, because we later realized that we had forgotten many essential things. Not to mention the seventeen gold watches that belonged to my father's boss, who was hiding from the Soviets and had left his possessions with various friends and acquaintances. These watches were hidden on the underside of the stove in our apartment, and my parents forgot all about them. This treasure would have come in handy later. I have often imagined the surprise and delight of the people who found them. I just hope they weren't German officers.

The next morning we packed our things in three knapsacks — a small one each for Mama and me and a big one for Papa — and we left without even locking the door behind us. First we went to the railway station, hoping to take the first train east. This was a waste of time; the trains had stopped running that morning. We then set out on the road to Minsk; my parents thought we could stay there until the end of the war. How naive that hope seems in retrospect, now that I know how long the war lasted and how quickly the Germans advanced.

So began our migration to the east. Hordes of displaced people were walking along with us and almost as many in the opposite direction. Packages, bags, and even suitcases lay along the side of the road, where they had been abandoned by tired refugees. From time to time, German planes flew over this defenseless mass of people and fired on them with machine guns. We took shelter in the ditch and, after the planes had passed, climbed back on the road again. Motor traffic was also heavy, as the Soviet army was retreating alongside us. The Russians didn't even try to defend Wilno, which fell to the Germans scarcely two days after the war began.

We had been walking for hours but each time my parents wanted to stop to rest or have a bite, I protested, "Quick! The Germans will catch us. We have to hurry!"

I was terrified of the German troops — quite rightly, too — but I couldn't keep up the strenuous pace and, after those first few hours, I was exhausted and had to ask to stop and rest more and more frequently.

After about twenty kilometres of this, Minsk was still far away. My mother started stopping Russian army vehicles and asking if they could take us. No one paid the slightest attention to this crazy woman at the side of the road; some even jeered. My father sat there silently, while I begged Mama to stop humiliating herself that way. But she kept on, and finally succeeded. A convoy of seven all-terrain vehicles had stopped by the side of the road. The commander gave in to my mother's pleas, although he warned us that we would each have to go in a separate vehicle. In panic, my mother started to tell the commander about people who had been separated in the First World War and were only reunited years after. He wouldn't listen.

"I am under orders to take this convoy to Minsk. It is impossible that any of the vehicles should be lost. Stop talking nonsense!" he said furiously.

By good fortune, one of the soldiers laid me down, fast asleep, on my mother's lap a few minutes later. I say by good fortune because of course the vehicles did become separated after all. It was very dark when we set off; in the distance we could hear the rumble of planes and muffled explosions. We couldn't tell where the bombs were falling, nor who was dropping them. Fortunately, I slept through almost the whole night. When I woke up from time to time, in terror, I quickly closed my eyes again so that I wouldn't hear anything, wouldn't see anything, would have nothing to think about. After a while, our car stopped. We could hear loud voices speaking in Russian, shouts and curses, and then we set off again. By now, we didn't know what direction we were going. In the middle of the night, our car stopped again and we were ordered to get out. We were in a little town. Before my mother could ask where we were and where the car with my father was, the convoy, now down to only four vehicles, drove off and disappeared into the darkness. The impossible had happened: the car with my father in it had gotten lost.

We found ourselves in a place called Borysov. That night nobody seemed to be sleeping. Squadrons of German airplanes were methodically bombarding the town and the neighbouring villages. Here and there houses were burning, and frightened villagers were trying to find their relatives and save their belongings. The streets were thronged with refugees and Soviet soldiers. Everyone was wandering around in shock, with no idea where to go. There was no food and nowhere to sleep. My mother was in despair and didn't know what to do. We walked along with everyone else through the streets and looked for Papa, but obviously there was no point in hoping for a miraculous reunion. We could only continue alone away from the Germans and their bombs.

We went to the station where, amazingly, the trains were still running. A train about to leave for Moscow was being mobbed.

"Moscow is a wonderful city! Let's go there!" cried Mama, and we began to elbow our way through the crowds to get on the already packed train. Suddenly Mama noticed a car reserved for mothers and children. Pushing me before her, she began to shout. "Let me through, I have a child. Make room for my child."

I didn't consider myself a child. I was a big girl, nearly eleven years old. I was mortified and furious at my mother for using me like that. As usual, she did as she pleased and we managed to get on the car for mothers and children, followed by two young men dressed in outdoor clothes and carrying large knapsacks. They were probably pretending to be my fathers.

The train started up and we began a journey of several days with almost no food, in the midst of a stinking crowd and wailing children — yes, there were also some "real" children.

From time to time the train would stop and we could buy cookies or cabbage rolls or other delicacies on the platform. There was also boiling water — *kipiatok* — which, with a little sugar, made an acceptable substitute for tea. My mother must have managed to buy some food in Borysov, for in the end we didn't starve to death. At the time, I paid no attention to these details. I was numbed by all we had been through and terrified of what might lie ahead.

We stayed on the train for a long time, days or even weeks, who knows. I remember no particular face from that long journey, no particular incident. We weren't allowed to get off in Moscow after all, not even just onto the platform, which was obviously a great disappointment to my mother. The train stayed in the station for a long time and then set off. No one knew where we were going and no one seemed to care. We were heading east, as far away as possible from the bombs and the war, and that was enough for us. Our immediate concerns — eating, drinking, bodily hygiene — kept us so occupied that we could, for a while, forget the horror of our situation.

Chapter 6

WE WERE LET OFF the train at Syzran, a little town on the banks of the Volga River. We were all herded into a school, empty for the summer vacation. Each family claimed a small territory, separated from the others by benches. We settled in as best we could, not knowing how long we would be there. School benches aren't the most comfortable things to sleep on, but the train wasn't either. We all did the best we could to make it through the night.

The next morning, Mama went to the market to look for food. We were running out of money, so she also wanted to sell her watch. Most of our money had been in Papa's wallet. We had no idea if or when we would ever find him again, but we still had to survive. I was left alone in our new "home", crowded with refugees, including many children. I played with them and with a kitten we found, but my main job was to guard our pitiful belongings from thieves. It hadn't taken us long to realize that we had packed our two knapsacks with useless stuff, and left behind the most important things in our apartment in Wilno. I still remember how my parents had not even locked the door behind them on that memorable day. It was as if they had known we would never return.

Mama came back from the market looking quite pleased with herself. She had managed to sell her watch and had bought a bit of food, which we dug into immediately. Best of all, she had found a place for us to stay. A woman had come up to her in the market and asked if she had been on the refugee train. Mama had answered yes, and the woman invited her to come to stay at her house. She thought Mama had a cultivated air about her, and was worried that if she didn't choose someone now, the authorities would make her take in a family she wouldn't like. She lived with her two teenaged daughters in an apartment with two bedrooms and a kitchen.

We eagerly packed our bags and moved to our new home, the first in a long series. Our room turned out to be only a little cubbyhole in the hallway, with a double bed that filled nearly all of the space. There was a window, but only a curtain separated us from the rest of the apartment. Our hostess and her two daughters lived in the big bedroom. The kitchen, which they let us use, was spacious and had a little balcony looking out over the street.

Our hostess was Latvian. Her husband had been arrested by the Soviet authorities after Russia had taken over the Baltic countries. She hadn't heard from him since she and their daughters had been deported to Syzran. Over the evenings spent together in the kitchen, she poured out her story to my mother. She would pace up and down like a madwoman, banging her head on the wall each time she reached it and crying, "Why? Why did this happen? What wrong did we ever do?"

This was the first time we met with Soviet reality and, for my mother, the first time she doubted the wonderful system in which justice and equality were supposed to reign supreme. Later, other stories would shake to the core her faith in the communist system.

We had our own little corner of the apartment and a real bed to sleep in. But we had none of the necessities of everyday life: no blankets or pillows, no forks or spoons, no pots or pans. You never think of these things, but you miss them sorely when they are not there. Our hostess lent us a few little everyday items, Mama bought two cotton blankets, and we began to live a "normal" life. But how different it was from the life I had known! Mama quickly found work as a cashier in a restaurant. She had never done this kind of work before, but at that time and in that place, if you knew how to use an abacus that made you an educated person who would have no trouble finding work. Since it was hard for us to cook in the apartment, we ate our main meal at the restaurant.

I spent my days at home with our hostess's daughters and their friends, who spoke Russian together. Since I didn't understand Russian, I would listen to their conversations without getting involved and, of course, without being able to join in. The girls were a little older than I was and they accepted me easily, probably because they knew I would be discreet. When they went out, I would spend hours on the balcony, looking at the street and the rare passersby.

One of my chores was to bring water from a well the next street over. I took a yoke with two buckets and, after waiting my turn, filled them about halfway, because I couldn't carry two full buckets of water back home. The women who came to the well were a talkative bunch and they tried to engage me in conversation, but I was stubbornly silent and hurried off as soon as I could. I could tell from their amused glances that they thought I was slow-witted, and indeed I did feel a bit that way. I couldn't communicate. And since I had no books, I couldn't read. I couldn't do anything. But I suppose I didn't feel particularly unhappy. The days went by, one after the other. Nothing much happened, and that in itself was a good thing.

A few days after we arrived, Mama sent a telegram to Aunt Liza and Uncle Yona in New York, telling them where we were and that we had lost Papa. She had remembered that Papa had asked her for their address in New York as we left the apartment in Wilno. It was usually Mama who wrote letters and Papa didn't know anyone's address.

"If by chance he remembers their address and decides to write to them, maybe that way we will find one another," Mama said, not really believing it.

It would be a real miracle, but we had to try. And the miracle happened. After a few days we got an answer from New York, with Papa's address, in care of the post office at Gorki. Gorki was a large town also on the Volga, a few hundred kilometres to the north. How happy we were!

We immediately sent a telegram to Gorki and waited impatiently for an answer. Days went by and no word came. It was strange and disturbing. All sorts of possible reasons for the delay, each more tragic than the last, ran through our minds — especially Mama's.

Two weeks later, on a beautiful afternoon, as I was sitting on the balcony looking over the street, I spied a familiar figure making his way to our house.

Yes, it was Papa, in person! He explained that he had been living quite a way from Gorki on a kolkhoz, a collective farm, and didn't go into town often. When other people from the kolkhoz went into town, he would ask them to stop by the post office to see if there was anything there for him. They would always come back saying no, there was nothing; they probably hadn't even checked. Finally, he went into Gorki himself and he found two telegrams waiting for him, one from New York and one from us. He didn't go back to the kolkhoz, but hopped on a boat going down the Volga to Syzran.

We went to Mama's restaurant together. Papa hid while I innocently asked her, "Guess who has come to visit us?" Mama nearly fainted from joy.

There was so much to tell! Papa had had a few misadventures as he wandered around looking for us on the road between Minsk and Borysov. He had no baggage, having lost his knapsack quite early on, and he looked suspicious to the Russian soldiers. They were actually taking him to a little wood to be shot as a German spy when, at the last moment, he managed to persuade them to take him to the commanding officer. The officer believed the story of this confused man who claimed to be looking for his wife and daughter. They wound up letting him go. When he got to Borysov, just as we had a few hours earlier, he hoped to find us there. But he too decided there was no chance, and got on a train for Gorki.

"What a miracle that we have been reunited, with help from America!" Papa and Mama exclaimed, one after the other. They weren't religious and certainly didn't believe in miracles, but they were very happy to be able to face the wartime difficulties together.

Now we had to think of the future. Our little cubbyhole in the apartment, with only one bed, was too small for the three of us. We had no clothes or shoes or blankets for the winter, and there was no way of getting any before the cold set in. Winter was very harsh in this region, but we were free to leave. Early in the war there was confusion everywhere, and you could still move from one place to another without special permission. We decided to head south, to warmer climes.

"I once read a book called *Tashkent: City of Bread*," said Papa. "Tashkent is supposed to be a warm place with plenty of food."

So, thanks to a book, we once again packed our bags. It wasn't hard to get our things together: we had very little, especially since Papa had lost the big knapsack. We went to the train station, where we quickly realized that leaving would not be so easy. There were no tickets, no schedules, no room in the cattle cars which were filled with people who would stop at nothing to prevent other passengers from getting on. A whole crowd was camped on the platforms, trying unsuccessfully to board a train, any train. We spent a few days at the station in the middle of this crush of people, hopelessly repeating our attempts to board each train that pulled in.

And once again a miracle occurred. The horde between us and one of the cars suddenly made way and let us through. How happy we were! We had managed to get the "inside people" on our side. The generous souls that had let us on were Jews from Lvov. They had probably seen that we were Jewish too and accepted us in solidarity. Once on board, we joined the others at the door and shouted that there was no more room ...

And that was the beginning of our long, exhausting journey to Tashkent, "City of Bread." I don't remember exactly how long it took. It was probably at least two weeks. In the railcar, our temporary home, there were two large wooden berths, with a wide passageway between them. We slept on the berths at night and sat on them during the day. There were little windows, so we could watch the countryside as we passed through.

Our train would often stop for hours on end, sometimes in the middle of nowhere. We never knew why the train stopped or had any idea how long the wait would be. We had to seize the opportunity at each stop to wash and take care of bodily needs. I was very self-conscious and was mortified each time I had to squat in front of the several hundred eyes that I imagined watching me from the train. Mama insisted that we keep ourselves clean under all circumstances. Each day we had to wash ourselves from head to toe. Papa refused, but whenever the train stopped Mama and I would wash, taking turns to shelter each other as best we could from the eyes of the curious. We were certainly the only ones on the train who washed so frequently and so carefully, which made it even more embarrassing.

The Lvov Jews on the train had money and food. They were cheerful and noisy and very sure of themselves. We felt like a miserable lot next to them. Once they gave us a little bag of sugar cubes to suck on while drinking tea, or rather hot water. They were delicious and temporarily stifled our hunger, but otherwise, we were almost always famished. It was no surprise we had little heart to admire the splendid, often exotic, countryside we were passing through. It changed constantly throughout our eastward odyssey. First came the vast forests of the Volga region; then mountains; then the land gradually grew flatter and the green faded: these were the Asian steppes; last was the desert, which seemed interminable. Everything there was the same greyish-yellow: the ground and the scarce vegetation, the low hills which stretched to the horizon, veiled in a light yellowish fog. It was monotonous and vaguely ominous. From time to time we would see caravans of camels which sometimes came close to our train. I loved animals, and one day I was foolish enough to offer some delicious grass to a young camel. Mistaking my intent, the filthy beast spat a disgusting greenish liquid all over me. Everyone around laughed heartily at my pitiful, offended look.

Ever since that day, I have been wary of camels.

The sun shone brightly and it was very hot in the train. My parents told one another happily that we wouldn't need warm clothing so it would be much easier to survive until the war was over.

No one tried to predict how long the war would last. It was much better that way; it would have been impossible to live knowing that four more harsh years of war lay ahead.

And that is how we came to Tashkent.

Chapter 7

THE TASHKENT TRAIN STATION was a crush of hundreds of passengers milling about and wondering what would become of them. Station officials came out of nowhere to give us contradictory information. Each person was handed a paper with a destination, this town or that village, determined by mysterious criteria. Only one thing was certain: no one would be staying in Tashkent. This was all under a blazing sun, with no protection from its intense rays. As usual, I stayed put with the baggage, while my parents went to find out where we would be going.

I sat on our bundles and looked around me. Everything seemed exotic and fascinating to me, quite different from anything I had seen before. Uzbek men moved about in quiet dignity, dressed in what looked like colourful quilts and wearing little embroidered caps on their heads. The women's dress was even stranger: long, gaudy pants worn under a slightly shorter dress, also brightly coloured. A long black mesh veil covered their faces and half of the body. A kind of shawl, also in vivid colours, hung down the back. There was no way of knowing what was underneath: a young woman or a grandmother, a beauty or a plain woman. You couldn't see a thing. They looked like big multicoloured dolls. The younger girls did not hide their faces under the black veils, but instead wore scarves on their heads, which they used to cover their faces whenever a man came near. Their shiny black hair was arranged in dozens of narrow braids that fell to the waist. I wondered how long it took to do their hair in the morning. I found out later that they washed and braided their hair only once a month.

After what seemed like forever, my parents finally returned with an official paper that assigned us to Zarkent, a tiny village near the border with the neighbouring Republic of Tajikistan. They hadn't been able to learn much about this village, and we didn't know if any other families would be going there too. But as no one had any better suggestions, we agreed. It turned out we were the only ones who were naive enough to accept. All the others managed to settle in bigger towns, and some even stayed in Tashkent. We weren't used to this way of life, where you got what you wanted by sidestepping official orders whenever you could.

The journey from Tashkent to Zarkent was long and hard. We rode in an arba, a wooden cart on two enormous wheels, which was pulled by a dromedary. Our Uzbek driver spoke hardly any Russian, so it was almost impossible to converse with him. It was a strange journey, but we were totally unable to appreciate the exotic sights. We crossed through desert lands that grew more mountainous the further we went along. From time to time, an Uzbek would pass riding on a donkey, often with his wife walking beside him, carrying packages on her head. Probably the donkey wasn't strong enough to carry a heavier load. Everything seemed to be happening in slow motion, as if in a fog. Sometimes in the distance we would see a single dromedary or several together, walking with a slow, dignified gait, their bodies swaying to the rhythm of some mysterious music. The occasional green patch would appear on the horizon, a little oasis where we would stop to drink a bit. Our driver would try to talk to us from time to time, but we couldn't understand a word. He gave up and began to sing — languid, wild songs that gave me goosebumps.

Our progress was slow under the burning sun, and we had the strange illusion that this journey would never come to an end.

But all things do come to an end. And our journey did too, at the little village of Zarkent. We were sent to see the head of the kolkhoz, apparently the most important figure in the village, the one who made decisions. Our arrival was a special event for the villagers. A crowd gathered in front of the building to see us, buzzing in astonishment at our strange appearance. They had never seen anyone like us. It also became clear almost immediately that, except for the bookkeeper, no one on the kolkhoz knew a word of the strange language we spoke. And even the bookkeeper wasn't much of an expert in Russian. Zarkent was in the back of beyond, on the edge of the civilized world or maybe even outside it. It was a tiny village, just a hamlet, nestled in a valley surrounded by mountains. There were ten or so little clay houses, with windows looking onto a courtyard, so that men could not see the women inside. The streets were like narrow passageways between the walls of the houses and the fences. Everything was coloured in ochre tones.

I couldn't imagine how my parents felt. Were they appalled? Or were they excited by the exotic locale? I had no idea. My feelings and concerns were like most children's. I wasn't very happy, because for some time I hadn't had any other children to play with or even just talk to. In Syzran, at the beginning of our journeys, I knew no Russian. Then, just when I was learning to speak a bit, we left. On the train, I was the only child in our car, and I had no books or toys. The world of adults didn't interest me much, so I had only my imagination to occupy me. And now I was thrust into an entirely strange and incomprehensible world, where no one knew a word of Russian. I was so incredibly bored that I decided to make up a new language. I invented words, gave each of them a meaning in Polish, and learned them by heart. My parents thought this was crazy behaviour, and they became concerned about my mental health.

They took steps to leave the village. They had long talks with Mr. Bookkeeper — or rather Comrade Bookkeeper — who could not understand why we didn't wish to stay in Zarkent for the rest of our lives. The argument that there was no Russian school left him unmoved; lots of children went to the Uzbek school, so why shouldn't I? We had been assigned to a fairly large room, we were given bread, what was the problem? But my mother was never one to give up a fight. When she showed him my notebook full of invented words as proof of my delicate state, he finally gave in. We were allowed to leave Zarkent and go to another village, called Czertak. The same driver as before took us there. The road to Czertak didn't seem long or exotic. I had become used to the landscape, the sun and the nostalgic songs of the coachman.

Czertak was scarcely larger than Zarkent, but it was near a town called Namangan. We rented a dark, cramped room, with a floor of beaten earth. It had no beds or other furniture, so we slept on the ground, on the cotton blankets we had bought in Syzran. That meant we had nothing to cover ourselves with, but fortunately at the end of August it was still quite warm. But how long would this last?

After a few days in Czertak, Mama came down with malaria, that terrible disease that was to torment us throughout our stay in Uzbekistan. Our whole situation was very disheartening. We also had to think of enrolling me in a school, now the summer vacation was ending. There was no Russian school in Czertak either, just a few Russian classes in an Uzbek school.

My parents decided that Papa would go to Namangan, about fifteen kilometres away, to see if we could move there. He left very early in the morning so that he could avoid the hottest part of the day and return by nightfall. I stayed in our horrible shack with my mother, who was running a high fever and seemed to be nearly unconscious. I gave her water, I put the blanket over her and took it off again, I tried unsuccessfully to get her to eat. I was terribly afraid that she was going to die. In anguish, I went out into the street again and again to see if Papa was coming. He didn't get back until very late, but he had good news. He had run into the Goldbergs, a couple we had travelled with on the train. They had avoided being sent to a tiny village, and had instead gone straight to Namangan. They both had work already and were staying in a room that they generously offered to share with us.

They were a young Jewish couple from Lvov, in their early twenties. I suspect that, as in the train, they were motivated by ethnic and national solidarity, but they might just have been trying to save some rent. At the time, I didn't really wonder about these things.

Their room was small and dreary too, with a dirt floor. As in all Uzbek houses, there was a tiny window overlooking the courtyard. Their bed stood opposite the door, while ours was against the wall on the left. Our presence made any intimacy difficult for the young couple and there was no privacy for us either. But at least we had a place to sleep, and even a bed, where my parents and I lay head to toe. I remember that the blanket was too short, and one or another of us was constantly tugging on it in the night. A cupboard for food and a few stools were all the other furniture in the room. Near the window there was a little stove with a single burner for cooking. Since we had very little to cook, there were no squabbles over the stove.

Grouped around the courtyard were other houses like ours, almost all of them occupied by refugees like us. Most were Jewish, but there were also a few Uzbeks and some very exotic-looking Jews from Bukhara, most of them professional shoe-shiners. The courtyard was always bustling. People ate outside, because the houses were overcrowded and very dark in the evening. Some people cooked outside, in a large cauldron over a small fire. Laundry was washed and dried in the courtyard, people washed themselves there, and shouted and quarrelled and sometimes even sang.

All anyone ever seemed to talk about was the scarcity of food. We were given tickets to buy bread, which was often all we had: 400 grams per day for children and office workers, 600 grams per day for labourers, and nothing at all for adults who weren't working. The bread was black and chewy, so dense that the 400 grams of the daily ration was such a little piece that it was very hard to keep from swallowing it in one gulp. Even today, when I see a one-kilogram loaf of bread, I am amazed at its size. As soon as we got home, the discussions about the bread ration would start. I always argued we should eat it all at once. That way, at least for an hour or two, we wouldn't feel hungry. Of course, my parents didn't agree. For them, the only question was whether it should be divided into two pieces or three. Two pieces would be bigger, but with three we could eat more often. This was a real bone of contention, and we returned to the subject again and again.

There were also tickets for sugar, but since there was rarely any in the shops we could buy it only two or three times a year. Instead, there was a kind of gingerbread that I grew very fond of, but we got so little that it would disappear almost immediately.

My father had found work as a bookkeeper. He gave

all his earnings to my mother, but it wasn't enough. I remember endless arguments between my parents, always the same. Mama would say we had so little to eat that sickness and death were at the door, and Papa would answer, "We have to live like everyone else. I give you everything I earn and you have to learn to manage. You don't expect me to start stealing, do you?"

Mama had no answer to that, but inside she was seething.

After these discussions, they would calculate and recalculate the figures, wondering how they could make do on their few pennies each month. There was only enough money to buy our bread rations, one bowl of soup each per day, and two kilos of carrots. Hunger gnawed at us constantly.

The soup was either a cabbage broth with a bit of flour added to thicken it, or else a kind of stew, with a few tiny pieces of meat. The stew, which we ate at the restaurant, wasn't as filling but it was much tastier and more nutritious. I savoured it slowly and ceremoniously: first the broth, which I pretended was my first course, and then the slivers of meat, my main course. One day, just as I had come to the high point of my meal, a beggar came up and asked if I had finished with my food. With enormous regret, I left him the best part of my meal. For a long time, I viewed this gesture as the most noble act of my life. But was I truly generous or just timid?

The carrots, which we stored in a corner of the room, featured in a tragicomic episode about a year after our arrival in Namangan. By that time, we were alone in the apartment. One night, I awoke with the strange sensation that the bed was rising up and then falling back down again. A noise as terrifying as the sound of a flight squadron overhead made the walls of the room shake. I jumped out of bed and ran into the courtyard, which was in an uproar. All the neighbours had run out of their apartments and were crying or praying. There had been an earthquake. I was in a panic and I begged my parents to come outside like everyone else. I was afraid that the roof would cave in on them. My father beckoned me over and said, "If we're going to die, let's at least eat the rest of the carrots. We don't want them to go to waste."

And with these words of wisdom, my parents sat down next to our pantry and began to munch on the miserable carrots, laughing uncontrollably. Of course, I didn't find the situation at all funny. I went and sulked in a corner of the room, which only made them laugh the harder. I learned a lot that night about the value of a sense of humour.

Luckily, nothing serious happened to us. There was only a new crack on the wall of the room to remind us of the excitement. But people had been killed or injured in the town, and some buildings had collapsed. Naturally, the newspapers mentioned none of this. The Soviet press always ignored events of this kind. We only learned of them by rumour, without ever being sure they had really happened. In my memory, the earthquake always reminds me of the story of the carrots.

Chapter 8

SEPTEMBER CAME, and it was time to enroll me in one of the schools in Namangan. In most of them, classes were in Uzbek, but a few used Russian. I entered Grade 5 in a Russian school. I was fairly proficient in Russian and could read and write. My accent wasn't too bad, and that's what usually causes problems for foreigners. There was only one sound — the Russian *l* — that gave me trouble and caused great hilarity among my schoolmates. When I meant to say *klas* (a class) they heard *kwas* (acid). But I learned to pronounce *l* in short order and soon no one could tell that Russian was not my mother tongue.

I was in with a group of children who had all known each other for a long time; I was a foreigner and felt very, very different from them. This was the third school I had attended, Russian was the third language of instruction for me, and Uzbek, which we studied as a foreign language, was my fifth language (after Polish, Yiddish, Lithuanian and Russian). It's not easy to be the new kid in school, and this time I was all alone. Hala was no longer by my side, and that was the hardest thing to bear.

All of these disruptions in my life — moving from one country to another, changing houses and languages and places — had made me very shy. I would never make the first move, but waited for an invitation, for others to ask me to play with them or be their friend. For quite a long time, I had no one to play with. I often spent recess alone in the classroom and walked home from school by myself. I wasn't happy, but I never spoke of this to my parents, who had much more important concerns and never asked me any questions. I was doing well in school — that was all that really mattered to them. They never even suspected that I might have other problems.

My new schoolmates seemed very different to me from those I had known before. Their clothing, games, and customs were quite strange to me. They also chewed gum constantly — either a hard black gum made from tree resin or else a soft white gum, which I later learned was actually paraffin. The girls would pass this treasure directly from mouth to mouth. Gum wasn't sold in stores, and I had no idea where or how I could get some. Since I had no friends, I couldn't chew gum like the others — one more reason to feel out of place.

There were, however, some satisfactions. No one could call me "Fatty" anymore, for I was now among the skinniest. The other children had immediately replaced my strange name with the Russian name Lena, quite common among girls. I kept this name until I left the Soviet Union.

Little by little, approaches were made and friendships formed. My first two friends were called Lusia and Wiera. Lusia was a lively, jolly girl, who cared little about lessons and homework. She often got poor grades, which didn't worry her in the slightest. She said she would be punished at home, but she was used to that and it didn't bother

her. "One spanking more or less, what difference does it make?" she would laugh.

Wiera was a tall, stocky girl with a pockmarked face. She often did poorly in school too. She lived with her older sister, who worked for the municipal committee of the Party. I remember this because when Wiera invited us to her house, we could eat all the bread, butter and jam we wanted. These were delicacies that I had not enjoyed for so long that I had almost forgotten what they tasted like.

I was very embarrassed when my friends came to our home and my mother offered them our usual meal — a thin cabbage broth thickened with a spoonful of flour or semolina. Despite our constant hunger, the old traditions of hospitality were not abandoned. Usually my friends would politely decline. Only bread, the staff of our survival, was never shared; everyone received the same paltry ration.

My class, and probably the others as well, was dominated by a group of kids known as "hooligans," who wouldn't listen to anybody or anything and kept the class in a permanent state of disruption. Few teachers could control their classes. Boys, and sometimes girls, would come and go whenever they felt like it, and shout and throw books and binders. It was practically impossible to teach under these conditions. In a whole year of French class, the only thing I learned was *un, deux, trois.* Only the geography teacher, who was also the school principal, maintained total silence in his class. We respected and feared him, though we didn't really know why.

Occasionally, a band of hooligans who had connections with local gangsters would invade the classroom in the middle of a lesson and, ignoring the teacher, attack one of the pupils. They would deliver a thrashing and then leave with no further ado. This happened to girls as well as boys, with complete equality. No one did a thing about it. Everyone was afraid of being stabbed somewhere in a dark corner of town.

One day, my friend Lusia did something that impressed me greatly. Hooligans had come into the schoolyard at recess asking, "Which one is Lusia?" There were two girls named Lusia in our class, my friend and another girl, tall and delicate, the daughter of a doctor from Odessa. "My" Lusia knew that the hooligans were looking for the other Lusia, but she went up to them anyway and said, "I'm Lusia, what do you want?" This was quite unexpected and she seemed so sure of herself that the boys, after hesitating a moment, turned tail and left without doing anything. When we asked her why she had done that, she shrugged and said, "I just wanted to see what would happen. I felt like having a bit of a fight, but it didn't work. They were too scared, the cowards!" It was a lesson for me, to see how courage could change the balance of power. I was taught this lesson again later, in a much more dangerous situation.

I learned a new word: *ogoltsi,* the name given to roaming boys who hung out with criminals. The term for the opposite was *domashnie maltchiki* — mama's boys — always used a bit scornfully. If a girl was suspected of being involved with *ogoltsi,* we left her alone.

So that was what my new school was like. My parents didn't have the slightest idea of what went on there, and I certainly didn't tell them anything. Perhaps I was afraid they would come to school and make a scene, which would have put me in a very difficult position. I really, really didn't want to stand out more than I already did. Or maybe it was simply that children do not usually tell their parents the details of their daily life. Either way, my parents were unaware of what went on at school the whole time we lived in Namangan.

Because of the war, we had no schoolbooks or exercise books. How could we study under such conditions? The town children often had textbooks from their older brothers or sisters or neighbours. I didn't. You could buy used books, but my parents didn't even have enough money to buy food. I had to work things out as best I could, borrowing books from a friend or staying in the classroom during recess to do my homework. It wasn't easy. I remember how happy I was when Mama bought me an old history textbook in Grade 6 or 7. It was used and worn, but it was mine. My marks in history went up immediately.

We used newspapers for scribblers, writing between the lines. It looked a mess and was hard to read, but there was never any shortage of newspapers, which were used for all sorts of things: to light fires, to roll cigarettes and as toilet paper. Maybe some people even read them ...

Gradually I got used to my new school and found a place for myself among the other children.

One fall day, we learned that the whole class was to go to a kolkhoz to help pick cotton, one of the main crops of the region. Cotton ripened fairly late in the year, in October, and a large part of the harvest rotted in the fields, as did many crops. People would do anything to get out of working in the fields on the kolkhoz. The pay was pitiful, and they found it more worth their while to tend their own little kitchen gardens, whose produce they could either eat or sell at a good price in the market. They also kept sheep, cows and chickens. Some even had little vineyards.

The land in Uzbekistan can be very fertile and the climate is excellent for all kinds of crops. Summers are long: for example, you can harvest two crops of corn, with time enough left to sow and harvest a carrot crop. But from April until November, not a drop of rain falls. Farmers used an ancient system for irrigating the fields. Hundreds of tiny ditches, called *aryks,* were dug in the field and linked to canals. The water came from a large canal upstream, fed by the Syr-Daria river. When you wanted to water your field, a dam had to be closed in the main canal, to direct the water towards your *aryks.* As can be imagined, this often caused fights among neighbours.

The kolkhoz we were sent to was quite far from Namangan and we had to get there by train. I remember how I made sure my mother would have no chance to kiss me goodbye at the train station. I was afraid my classmates would make fun of me, and I didn't want to stand out.

After travelling several hours on the packed train and then walking for a few kilometres, we finally arrived at our kolkhoz. We were twenty girls, along with our teacher, all housed in one little room. When we lay down for the night, our heads against the wall and our feet towards the middle, we filled the entire floor. Anyone who got up in the night to pee couldn't help but step on the others.

Very early in the morning, we were woken up and led to the fields. We weren't fed until we got there, usually on thin broth thickened with rice or flour. We hardly had time to swallow our soup before we were put to work. Cotton grows on medium-size bushes and it's ready to be picked when the pods burst open into a little cotton ball. We were expected to pick these little balls and put them in a sack. Once the sack was full, we would take it to a scale, where an Uzbek man would weigh it and mark the amount next to each girl's name.

We didn't enjoy this work, but since we were under constant threat of all kinds of punishment, such as going without food if we didn't pick enough cotton, we did whatever we could to have a large enough amount marked next to our name. The best trick was to distract the man at the scales and then fill our sacks with cotton that had already been weighed. If the same cotton could be weighed several times, we would get the extra credit. This tactic wasn't very honest, but I don't recall feeling guilty. No one at the kolkhoz seemed to have any idea what was going on, and I suspect that they themselves were quite proud of their harvest that year!

In the rare moments we weren't supervised, we sat down at the edge of the field and warmed ourselves in the sun, not too hot at that time of year. We would check one another for lice which, in our living conditions, spread rapidly. This was an intimate activity, an act of love and devotion among close friends. As we picked lice, we would tell each other little secrets or scraps of gossip. Often we would sing. The girls knew lots of old folk songs, and also modern songs, many of them about the war, celebrating the heroism of the Soviet soldiers and the faithfulness of their wives. Russians loved to sing and they sang very well. Whenever young people were together, they would always end up singing at some point. Singing was a new experience for me and I sang very badly, but I quickly grew to enjoy it.

When our day of work was done, we would go into the village to trade whatever we could for food. The only thing I had to offer was a piece of soap my mother had given me with strict instructions to wash myself every day from head to foot. I quickly forgot these instructions. The water in the *aryks* was cold and dirty. Nobody washed, except perhaps their hands and faces, and not even that every day. My piece of soap, quite a desirable commodity in those days, was cut into three smaller pieces and traded for flour cakes. After that, I had nothing left to offer, but the other girls had more and continued to trade off various parts of their wardrobe.

From time to time a package would arrive from someone's family. Depending on each girl's circumstances, it might contain treats or just a piece of dry bread, all crumbled away. I was one of the ones who received a package of dry bread, but I knew what a great sacrifice that must have represented for my parents. Most of the girls were very generous and shared their packages with their closest friends. Only Alla, a pretty girl who was always well-dressed and whose father worked for an important committee, would gobble her treats all by herself, hiding as best she could behind her open suitcase. Our scorn and loud comments had no effect until the end of our stay there. On the last day she offered her neighbours a few leftovers from her feast. But one after the other, the girls politely refused. We were hungry, but the satisfaction of teaching her a lesson was sweeter than any treat.

Even in hungry times like those, pride and dignity could sometimes win out.

We were overjoyed when the time came to leave the kolkhoz, and happy and proud to have done our bit for our country. We arrived home in a pitiful state — dirty, scrawny, lice-ridden, and exhausted. Mama looked at me aghast. Instead of hugging me, feeding me and tucking me into bed, she boiled a huge pot of water and began to clean me. The delousing took a long time. My mother said that in her whole life she had never seen so many lice. I was mortified.

Chapter 9

AFTER MONTHS OF GOING without, my mother decided something had to be done. She threw herself into making cabbage rolls to sell at the market. Maybe it was because Papa and I sampled too much of the stuffing when she was preparing the rolls, but the project was a failure.

But Mama didn't give up. Figuring you had to go where there was food, she got a job doing laundry in an institute for blind children. She was entitled to a meal in addition to her wages, which left a bit more food at home for Papa and me. After a little while, she was allowed to bring home a pot of soup for us. I'll never forget watching poor Papa, already grown thin and weak, waiting impatiently at the doorstep for Mama to arrive with the pot of soup — or rather, for the pot to arrive with Mama!

We now had the room all to ourselves. The Goldbergs had left. The farewells were not fond ones; predictably, the arrangement had gradually soured. It was partly my fault. One day I had been sent to the store to buy the ration of bread for all five of us. On the way, I stopped at the public baths. I hung my coat up in the cloakroom and went to wash. When I returned, my coat was still there but the bread tickets had disappeared. It was at the beginning of the month, so my parents had to somehow arrange for bread for five people. I have no idea how they managed this. I still wonder what they did.

There were special stores that did not require bread tickets, but the bread cost a lot more there. This bread was called "commercial bread". To buy some, you had to have money and you had to go stand in line very early in the morning, or even sometimes in the middle of the night, and then wait for hours.

I have a clear memory of the Goldbergs' preparations for their departure. Mrs. Goldberg — Genia — sold everything that could be sold, including a big iron pot called a *shougoune,* which had a special shape, very narrow at the bottom, so that it could be pushed down into the stove. Once she had decided to sell it, Genia started to pee in it, delighted with the idea that the person who bought it would be eating out of a pot she had peed in. How bizarre this seemed to me. I am still filled with disgust when I remember it.

We weren't alone for long in our room. One day Mama burned her arm fairly badly with a pot of hot soup. After a few days in hospital, she returned with a new tenant. Ludmilla was a single woman about the same age as my parents. She had a slight limp and received ration tickets as a disabled person. For these, she had work to do at home. Her job was to make balls out of piles of tangled cotton yarn. She had to turn in quite a lot of these to earn her bread tickets each month, so she hired me to help her. That is how I earned my first wages — 16 rubles. I was very proud. Of course I gave it all to my mother so she could buy a little bit more food.

Mama's job at the institute for blind children didn't solve all our problems. First, it was hard work. Mama had to do all the laundry for about a hundred children, and she wanted everything to be spotlessly clean. This was impossible, especially after she burned her arm. What's more, she felt great pity for those poor children and couldn't bear to see how the directors of the orphanage shamelessly stole the food intended for the children and sold it on the black market.

They offered her a share in the stolen goods, which of course she refused. The situation had become unbearable. She was determined to leave and figure out another way to make ends meet. The solution came to us because most Uzbeks, despite intense Soviet propaganda, remained devout practising Muslims. They did not eat pork, but a typically Soviet regulation still required each kolkhoz to raise pigs.

Needless to say, it wasn't a popular job, so when a pigkeeper's "position" came up, Mama had no trouble getting hired. She said that a small family like ours could survive with no problem in a place where twenty or so pigs were raised, and we need never be hungry again.

We left Ludmilla the apartment, and moved to the pigkeepers' house in a kolkhoz about three kilometres from town — quite a way from my school. This move took place on April 16, 1942. It was my mother's birthday. I remember that I had thought long and hard of what present I could give her. Finally I had the idea of scouring the streets for apricot pits. I broke them open to remove the kernel, which tasted like almonds. I gave my mother a whole box of these treats. She was very touched, and I discovered that it is infinitely more gratifying to give than to receive.

In the kolkhoz, we lived in an immense room, like a reception hall or a ballroom, in the former home of an Uzbek *bey* (a rich landowner). There were still a few vestiges of the old decorations: colourful paintings on the wall, mosaics on the marble floor, niches that we used for closets or shelves. A little metal stove in the corner was used for cooking, but wasn't nearly big enough to heat the house in winter.

Our home was at the back of a large courtyard surrounded by little houses of the Russian *isba* type, which had been built more recently. They weren't as lovely as ours, but they had big stoves that kept them warm in winter. I only remember two of the families that lived there: a Bessarabian Jewish couple with two children a little younger than I, and an old Polish couple, Mr. and Mrs. Bojarski, who tended a weather station in the far corner of the courtyard. The Bojarskis were very kind and would sometimes help us out. Mrs. Bojarski visited from time to time to talk with us in Polish, which she had almost completely lost even though it was her native language .

On the other side of the street, on a huge lot, stood the service buildings, including a huge shelter where silkworms were raised and, at the very back, the pigsty. There was also a little shed with a cauldron, where we could cook the pigs' food.

The former pigkeeper had outlined our tasks: twice a day, the pigs had to be fed and watered, one bucket of food and one bucket of water each; and at least three times a week, the sty had to be cleaned out. But early on, a multitude of problems arose, which could not have been foreseen. The most serious was the irregular delivery of feed for the pigs. The managers of the kolkhoz were all Uzbeks and despised pigs, so they often "forgot" that the pigs needed to be fed.

Up until then, of course, our sole experience of pigs had been a slice of ham or a few pork chops purchased at the butcher's. At first glance, the job didn't seem that difficult. Unfortunately, Papa, a true scientist at heart, insisted on studying the problems of pig farming and to this end had bought a few books on the subject. According to these books, pigs required great care: they had to have fresh air regularly and be given a bath at least once a week. But our pigs scorned this expert opinion. They hated to be washed and put up a fight whenever we tried it. On the other hand, they really enjoyed the one walk they were ever allowed, and it took us hours to get them all back in the sty. They ran everywhere, grunting and wagging their tails. The experience was so harrowing that we quickly abandoned the experts' recommendations!

Around this time, I began to suffer serious attacks of malaria. When I felt one coming on, I would hurry to my bed, and only after several hours of a high fever, chills and sweats could I even attempt to struggle up again. Mama was afraid I would not live; each attack left me weaker than the last. One time, certain that I was about to die, she phoned Papa to tell him to send for a doctor. The whole day long, she watched for Papa to come, but he returned alone. No doctor was willing to go so far to treat a patient. But my father had brought back a real treasure for me: a little pouch of sugar. This sugar gave me strength, and perhaps it even saved my life!

Several folk remedies were tried out, and one in particular left me with a very unpleasant memory: I had to drink my own urine. I resisted this like the very devil, but it wasn't easy to oppose my mother when the life of her only child was at stake. To make it easier for me, she added some grated apple to the glass of fresh urine. Weeping and cursing, I forced the disgusting mixture down. That was the first and the last time, for I never agreed to it again, although the malaria attacks recurred throughout the time we were in Uzbekistan.

Chapter 10

OUR LIVES HAD CHANGED. We were no longer hungry. Mama was right: the small amount of food we took for ourselves from the pigs' ration was enough.

We were sent bags of corn bran mixed with whole kernels and meal. We crushed the kernels into flour in a sort of mortar set in a hollowed-out tree trunk. Then we sifted the flour to remove the uncrushed kernels. It was long, tiring work, but it gave us a lot of corn flour. We could make a sort of *kasha* by boiling the leftover kernels.

Whole truckloads of melons, tomatoes or carrots would arrive for the pigs. Most of this produce was rotten, but we went through the deliveries carefully and always managed to find some good enough to keep for ourselves. Sometimes a dead dromedary or horse was also sent, but Mama was afraid to use this meat. One time only, she cut off a piece of a dromedary thigh. The meat was delicious and, miraculously, we did not die of food poisoning.

Deliveries were very irregular. We could go for several days without receiving anything. The pigs screamed in hunger, and often we were afraid to go into the sty. At those times we would go the kolkhoz orchard and gather food for the pigs: grasses, fallen fruit, whatever we could find. A lot was needed to fill their stomachs. We also filled our own with fruit that was underripe or else overripe, which often made us sick.

We soon got to know the personality of each pig and we gave them nicknames. One delicate sow that bore a few days of hunger with calm dignity was called Madame. There were also Sad, Stingy, Dirty and so on.

After a while, we began to raise chickens as well. This was my idea, and I was very proud. One fine day, when I was weak after a bout of malaria, Mama decided to buy a chicken to make a broth for me. She returned from the market with a fine-looking hen, black with red and white speckles. I took pity on the poor animal and begged my mother to spare its life. I argued that we could use the many nutritious eggs it was sure to lay. Mama agreed, but from that day on the hen's life depended entirely on its egg production. The hen seemed to understand and regularly laid one egg a day. Impressed with this performance, we decided to buy another hen. This one was yellow and not as productive as the first; it only laid an egg every other day.

We gradually became used to our new way of life, which was hard but allowed us to eat nearly our fill. We especially enjoyed the fruit Mama and I stole from the kolkhoz orchard, which was guarded by an old and very pious Uzbek man. Several times a day, he would unroll a little rug, turn towards Mecca and say his prayers. During this time, we could gather fruit without getting caught. The best of the bounty were the peaches — enormous, juicy and very sweet. I have never seen such fine peaches since. Papa, of course, did not take part in these raids, but he would eat the fruit greedily and say, "Never forget: without your mother, we would have starved to death. We owe our lives to her."

Shortly after coming to the kolkhoz, we planted a kitchen garden in the plot next to the pigsty, which had lain fallow for years, fertilized all that time by pig manure. People told us that pig manure was not good for plants; nothing would grow, everything would wither. But despite our inexperience, we had excellent harvests. We grew all sorts of plants: corn (which gave two crops a year), pumpkins, melons, cantaloupes (which grew very fast and could be used as a vegetable), carrots, tomatoes, eggplant, soybeans — everything but potatoes, which wouldn't grow in the heavy clay soil. And gardening was much more enjoyable than working in the pigsty.

Unfortunately, our garden made the neighbours envious, and our prettiest pumpkins began to disappear. I was furious at having my "babies" taken from me. I decided to catch the wicked thief, so I hid in the big shed where silkworms were raised and settled in to watch over the garden. I fixed my eyes on one of the finest pumpkins and I waited. I had to wait a long time and I must have dozed off for a few minutes, because all at once I realized that the pumpkin was gone. I wept tears of rage, but we never found out who the thief was. From time to time other produce would disappear.

Now we had enough to eat, but we still didn't have enough money to buy clothing and other things that don't grow in a kitchen garden. So Mama decided we should sell some of our harvest. One morning she gave me a fine big pumpkin and sent me to the kolkhoz market to sell it, telling me in no uncertain terms not to accept less than five rubles for it. I didn't feel comfortable as a saleswoman, and when a woman offered me three rubles, picked up the pumpkin and calmly walked off, I did nothing to stop her. On the way home, I felt deeply ashamed and afraid of what my mother would do, but she merely took the money without a word. She never sent me to market to sell things again.

Just as we knew little of how to raise pigs, we were totally ignorant of how they reproduced. When, for the first time, one of our sows gave birth, we weren't in the least prepared for the event.

Unfortunately, this sow was not a good mother, or perhaps she was really hungry that morning. In any case, when we got to the pigsty, we found the remains of her poor litter; not one piglet had survived! We learned the hard way that we must keep better track of the females' condition, count the weeks of their pregnancies, feed them well, and most important, be there when they gave birth.

The second sow to drop a litter was Madame. As she had been well fed till the end of her pregnancy, she was bursting with milk and her teats were swollen. Perhaps we had tried too hard to do the right thing and overdone it. Papa and I attended the delivery. Madame gave birth to ten piglets, nine of them healthy and one that wasn't breathing. Papa immediately looked in one of his books to find out what to do in such a case, and we dunked the piglet first in a bucket of hot water and then in a bucket of cold water. After a few dips, the piglet started to breathe again and immediately crawled up to its mother's teats. It's amazing how newborns know from the start what they want and where to get it! Early the next morning, when we went out to the pigsty, we found one of the piglets dead, smothered under Madame. With heavy hearts, we buried it in the yard. To this day, I cannot understand why we didn't eat that poor piglet! It would have made a succulent meal, the best in five years of war! Sometimes human beings are totally irrational.

We decided to set up a watch around Madame and her offspring, to stop it from happening again. I remember one of those nights when, alone with the pigs for a few hours, I was terrified by the slightest noise in the darkness. After all, I was only twelve years old. When Papa came to take over, he asked me if I had been afraid. Of course, I denied it indignantly.

Madame's teats were so swollen that the piglets couldn't feed, so we put the piglets in a separate stall and got some baby bottles and cow milk to feed them. The piglets quickly figured out how to suck at the bottles and as soon as Mama or I came to the sty, they would crowd around the entrance, jostling and grunting cheerfully. At the same time, we tended to Madame, applying cold compresses to her swollen teats. After a few days, everything was put right and the family could be reunited.

The piglets were very cute and I came to look forward

to feeding them, walking them, and playing with them. I found out how interesting it can be to look after animals.

It was about this time that our Number 1 hen stopped laying. She started wandering around in an agitated state, cackling strangely. I thought maybe she was sick so I went to ask advice from Mrs. Bojarski. Our neighbour knew all there was to know about farm animals, and I had absolute confidence in her. She herself had an adorable goat that had just had two extraordinarily beautiful kids. All the children around the courtyard loved to come and watch and pet the kids. I liked to visit Mrs. Bojarski, especially in winter, because her little house was kept snug and warm by a big Russian stove, while our enormous room was always icy cold.

Mrs. Bojarski examined my hen and explained that it wanted to have chicks. I was very excited! I made a comfortable nest and put some eggs in it, and the hen sat on them. I looked after her extra tenderly, I was so worried that something might go wrong. One night I was woken up by strange sounds: cracking noises and feeble chirps. I knew what that meant! I leaped out of bed and ran to Mrs. Bojarski's house to ask for help. It was three o'clock in the morning, but the kind woman got up without a complaint and came over to supervise. Eight beautiful downy yellow chicks were hatched, three hens and five roosters. Quite the family!

The chicks grew rapidly, and I was as proud as if they had been my own children. A few weeks later, I had to face an upsetting task — I had to kill one of the young roosters with my own hands to make a nourishing broth for Mama, who was once again suffering a severe bout of malaria. I cut off its head with an axe, and the decapitated chicken began to run around and jump in the air. I burst into tears and ran off, so I wouldn't have to see it.

In that summer of 1942, the news from the front was not encouraging. The Germans' siege of Moscow had ended but they were still not far from the city, and Stalingrad had been under siege for several months. Everyone believed that if these two cities were to fall to the enemy, the war would be lost; but no one dared to say this aloud for fear of being arrested for their defeatist attitude or, worse yet, for being a German spy. Anything could happen. You only confided your thoughts to your closest friends, and even then you had to be careful. I remember one time everyone was discussing the situation at the front and the certainty of victory, and a heavy silence fell when a girl said, "Don't count your chickens before they're hatched." No one turned her in, but anyone could have. If she wasn't confident of victory, that meant that perhaps she did not want victory, and her parents surely thought and talked the same way ...

The war bulletins on the radio and in the newspapers were always in the most positive language — for example, "Our troops have retreated to new strategic positions." You never knew what to make of them. That is why, towards the end of 1942, when it was announced that the German army had been surrounded in Stalingrad and then that Germany had surrendered unconditionally, we didn't dare to believe it was true. We were still puzzled and uncertain about the outcome of the war. But not everyone in the USSR hoped for a Soviet victory, and some even hoped that the Soviet Army would be defeated. Throughout 1942, rumours swirled that *basmatches,* the Uzbek nationalists, were planning an uprising to regain their independence; according to these rumours, when the time came, all "whites" — Russian, Polish, and Romanian alike — would have their throats slit. My father began to plan our escape across the mountains on the Afghan border, but without a map or any familiarity with these steep, snowy mountains, we would never have made it. Luckily for us, the great Russian offensive put an end to these rumours of rebellion.

It was during this time that I began to realize that the great friendship among the peoples living together in the Soviet empire, much proclaimed by the government and the Party, was in reality just an illusion. In fact, everyone hated everyone else. In Uzbekistan, there was an insulting nickname for every minority: the Koreans, who were quite numerous, were called Chinks; the Jews were called Yids. Ethnic origin was important; it was written on all our papers and was impossible to change. I remember how much trouble my father had getting "Polish" put on his passport. The registry official told us that our family name, Flutsztejn, was not Polish but Jewish. Papa argued that he had been born in Poland, but the official replied, "If you had been born in a stable, would that make you a horse?"

I don't know how my father finally managed to have us recognized as Polish, but had he not, we would have found it very difficult to return to Poland after the war.

A sad letter arrived from New York from Uncle Yona, telling us that Aunt Liza had died at the age of forty-eight. My cousin Hala was thirteen years old then, an age when a girl still needs her mother. I was grief-stricken. I couldn't imagine that, after the war when we were all together again in Miedzeszyn, Aunt Liza would not be there with us. When Papa came home from work and read the letter, tears sprang to his eyes. This was the first time I had seen him cry, and it made me even sadder. Papa and his sister Liza had loved one another dearly.

Older men and foreigners were not at risk of being sent to the front, but they were soon called up to work in the arms factories. This was called mobilization to the labour front. My father was mobilized and sent to work in a factory in the Urals. Life became much harder for Mama and me, since we now had to shoulder all the work in the piggery.

Soon we began to receive unhappy letters from Papa. He had to work hard from morning to night, never had enough to eat (no fruits or vegetables, a ration of only 600 grams of bread a day), and had no money to buy food at the market. Once again, Mama came up with a solution: we would send him packages of *uriuk* — dried apricots — to sell at the market. This was a brilliant idea. In central Russia, fruits were a rare commodity and were much in demand. Papa's daily life improved and he was able to send us some of the money he made.

Now we could buy other food beyond what was delivered for the pigs, such as milk, sour cream and even fat. I will never forget the day when Mama bought a little pot of oil. It was thick and black, actually quite disgusting. But it was still a fat, and we hadn't had any for a long time. This treasure was set out on the windowsill and one day I carelessly knocked it over, smashing the pot to smithereens. I was devastated and terrified of what my mother would do. But as she set to cleaning up the mess, she only said, "It was poison anyway, not fit to eat!"

Another of Mama's experiments was an attempt to make sugar. We had ration tickets for sugar but there was never any in the stores, and at the market it was very expensive. Mama decided that she would produce sugar from mulberries. Mulberry trees grew plentifully everywhere, since the leaves and branches were used to feed the silkworms. I picked two large buckets of mulberries. We pressed them and set the juice to boil over a low fire, expecting that once it boiled down we would have real sugar, perhaps not white but still usable. Unfortunately, what remained was only a thick syrup, which hardened into a totally inedible lump.

So, in the summer of 1942, we were settled in at our kolkhoz, the pigs were under control, the vegetables were growing well, and we were looking forward to a fine harvest. Papa wrote happy letters home, promising to return soon. Life was a bit easier, especially for my mother. School was out, and I had more time to help her on the farm.

This quiet time was short-lived. One morning, the neighbours woke us early, shouting that our garden had been invaded by a herd of cattle. We finally understood why the large lot around the pigsty had been left empty — this was where the herders stopped when they brought their herds down from the mountain pastures. We rushed out to save our rows of vegetables.

The scene must have been hilarious: Mama and I in our nightclothes, brandishing sticks, rushing and screaming at the beasts to chase them off, under the mocking eyes of the Uzbeks who, far from helping us, were splitting their sides laughing. The skirmish lasted several hours. I was on the verge of giving up more than once, but Mama — never. We finally drove the animals off and took a moment to catch our breath before trying to repair the damage. Our garden was saved, but at what cost! This really brought home to us how the fruits of our labour could be wiped out from one day to the next. We were exhausted and disheartened.

One morning when we went out to the pigsty, we found the sow we called Stingy lying on the ground, dead. Mama called the veterinarian and asked him to come to determine the cause of death. He was a friendly, young man. After a careful examination, he told us, "She died of a heart attack, so you can safely eat the meat. But for the kolkhoz administration I'll write that she died of an infectious disease and had to be buried immediately."

He left, wishing us happy eating. The next day, when

Mama went to pick up the death certificate, she found the vet and his wife having breakfast. They invited her to join them. To Mama, their meal was a glorious feast but, knowing that her only child had not tasted such things for several years, she couldn't really enjoy it. They understood her hesitance and made up a little package of ham, cheese and white bread for her to take home to me. I gobbled it all down in a trice, with Mama looking on, amazed at how generous people can be.

"In hard times, you discover people's real nature," she said. "Some turn meaner and greedier, while in others, hardship brings out only kindness and generosity." She had met far too many of the first kind!

So we now had quite a lot of meat. Part of it we salted and hid in a cask in the basement. We gave some away to friends and neighbours, and ate the rest, not even pausing to worry about the effect on our delicate stomachs. We had pork chops dripping with fat at every meal. This was the first time in five years of war that we had had so much meat. Sadly, it didn't last long; someone discovered our hiding place and the salted meat disappeared one day without a trace.

During this time, we discovered that the orchard guard — the one whose frequent prayers had allowed us to steal fruit from the orchard — was not quite as devout as he seemed. One evening, he appeared suddenly in the middle of our pork chop dinner and demanded his share, although he knew quite well what kind of meat it was. Mama said nothing but served him a large plateful, and he wolfed it down.

Chapter 11

AUTUMN CAME. It was time to go back to school, but I had lost my enthusiasm. I hadn't seen my friends for the whole summer, and I was sure they had forgotten all about me. I didn't feel like starting all over again at square one. Once more, I felt that I was totally different from my schoolmates, especially since most of the few children I knew at the kolkhoz did not go to school. Their parents thought school wasn't that important. It was too far to go and too much trouble, and anyway, the children didn't have the right kind of clothes. They could go back to school when the war was over. It was true that we had to walk more than three kilometres to get to school, and on the way Uzbek boys would throw stones at us and insult us and there was no one to defend us. In the summer the ground was so hot that it burned our feet. In the fall and winter, on the other hand, it was muddy and our feet were always sodden. I had no shoes and nothing suitable to wear. Usually I wore what had been my nightgown in Wilno. It was green with little pink and yellow flowers, and I tied it at the waist with a piece of string.

In these circumstances, then, I would have been happy to have a break from school. My mother did not agree: war or peace, cold or famine — it made no difference; you had to continue your education. Mama and I had a terrible fight. I cried and ran out of the house, and she ran after me. Finally I had to give in. Resentful and red-eyed, I put on my so-called dress and went to school. That very evening, I admitted to Mama that she had been right. My school friends and I had greeted each other warmly and told endless stories of our summer vacation. I felt after all that I did fit in at school, and I was quite happy.

There was a new teacher in charge of our class. Raïssa Pavlovna was a pretty, lively young woman, who immediately charmed everyone, even though she taught mathematics and physics, two subjects that most of us hated. It was like a miracle — everyone wanted to please the new teacher. Our class, which the previous year had been the rowdiest in the school — all the teachers said so — was now a model of discipline. No more playing hooky; we sat quietly on our benches and willingly worked hard to earn the best marks we could. Raïssa Pavlovna was a true teacher: she never scolded us, but had only to give us a look to make us behave. Even today I am amazed at the feat she accomplished. She transformed a group of ruffians, uncontrollable and impossible to teach, into a class of normal, studious pupils.

This was when I first made friends with Lena Prokofieva, who was to become my best friend. Lena was a short girl, not particularly pretty. She was always dressed very neatly; her clothes were simple and poor, but impeccably mended, washed and ironed. With two thick braids wound around her head, her pale face calm and determined, she always held her head high. Lena had always been one of the best students, even at the time when being a good student was scorned by our classmates. Her copybooks were always neat. She was different from the others, but that fact didn't seem to bother her. What impressed me most about her was her dignity and courage. Often after school, a gang of hooligans would chase us and pull our hair and shove us around. All the girls would run away, crying. All but Lena, who didn't even change her pace. Tiny, her head held high, she kept on walking as if nothing was amiss. Her attitude flummoxed the boys, and they left her in peace.

How did she come to have such self-assurance and dignity? I don't know, but she impressed me greatly. I wanted to be like her, but I didn't have her courage.

Lena came from a large family. Her parents were very strict, especially with the girls. I remember that her elder sister had been driven from the home. I don't know what crime she had committed — that was a family secret. Lena's father was a bookkeeper and her mother worked as a cleaning lady. Today I am certain that the family had been deported from central Russia or Ukraine, during the Stalinist purges; but at the time, this was never spoken of, and I didn't even know where they had been before coming to Uzbekistan.

At the same time, I began to spend time with two other girls — Zina Uspienskaya, a cheerful blond Ukrainian girl whose parents were both veterinarians, and Liza Kim, a little Korean girl who was very gifted in sciences. My friends even came once or twice to the kolkhoz, so far from town. These great friendships had taken some time to develop, but when the time came to leave Uzbekistan I was deeply saddened to say goodbye to my friends.

It was the winter of 1942, a year and a half since the war had broken out between Germany and the Soviet Union. Following a treaty between General Sikorski and the Russian government, delegations of the Polish government were set up throughout the Soviet Union to look after the Polish people who had been scattered across this vast territory. These delegations received gifts of clothing and food from the Americans. At first, we had no contact with the delegations, but rumour had it that the few who grabbed all the jobs distributed some of the goods among their own friends and relatives and sold the rest at the markets. We didn't know whether this was true or not, but it seemed likely.

Our clothing was pitiful. I have already mentioned my nightgown, which had served me well but was now beginning to tear in several places. Mama's dress was a jute bag with holes cut in it for her head and arms — the sack the pig meal came in! She had dyed it blue and tried to pretty it up a bit. It wouldn't have been so bad without the big black printing on her behind. We had no warm clothing for winter, not even proper shoes.

So Mama decided to go to the delegation to ask for help. There she met several elegant, well-coiffed women, with pale, smooth hands. They treated her with snobbish politeness, but they didn't send her home empty-handed. She brought back a few yards of fabric and a pair of shoes for me. The shoes were the stuff of dreams: they were made of shiny burgundy leather, with a fringed flap. Unfortunately, they were too small for me. I was willing to make any sacrifice to wear them, like the little mermaid in Andersen's famous tale, but I couldn't stand to have them on my feet for more than fifteen minutes. Mama told me to go the delegation to exchange them, and I did go. I stood for an hour in front of the building, not daring to enter. And yet I really wanted to have something lovely that the others didn't have! But there was nothing for it: I was too shy to go in. We had to sell the shoes to buy another pair for me, but the new pair wasn't nearly as nice and I was disappointed.

With the fabric, Mama made me a black-and-white checked skirt and a yellow blouse. I was relieved that I didn't have to wear that ragged nightgown anymore.

Although our house was quite far from town, we had made a few friends, almost all of them Polish Jews. Some of these people remained our friends for life. There were a few children my age, which made these relationships more interesting to me. I was terribly lonely in my isolation, and I needed to feel I belonged, that there was someone I could count on. I would so much have liked to have a bigger family, a sister or a brother. But alas, I didn't!

Even in these hard times, we kept up the old traditions of Polish hospitality. Visitors were always asked to share our meal. We had good soup, grains, vegetables — things that were often lacking in town. Again, only bread was not shared, for everyone got more or less the same amount. During our time at the kolkhoz, we would occasionally have famished visitors who came mainly to fill their bellies. When we went to visit our friends in town, we would bring vegetables from our garden. These gifts were always appreciated — much more than a bouquet of flowers!

A frequent visitor at that time was a Warsaw lawyer, an unmarried man who was terribly worn down by the years of war. Each time he came he would share a meal with us. Sometimes he would spend the night; we had room and the town was far. When I think about it now, I wonder if there were not other, ulterior motives. At the time, I never considered this. We often had visitors, both men and women, who would come for dinner and spend the night.

The lawyer's visits stopped suddenly, and we were worried. Had he fallen sick? Or had something worse happened? One day our neighbour, who worked at a factory in town, told us that one of her friends had bought a lovely handmade woollen sweater from a Polish lawyer. Mama immediately went to look inside the wooden box she kept under her bed. Sure enough, her beautiful woollen sweater that Aunt Liza had knit for a goodbye present was missing. Mama had never dared to wear the sweater, as it was too beautiful. She had been saving it to sell if necessary. We had been saving various small treasures, items of clothing, for even harder times, for the "black hour", as an old Polish expression goes. And now one of these precious treasures had been stolen by a so-called friend! It was hard to say what was sadder — the loss of a friend or the loss of our illusions.

After the war, I happened to see this man on the streetcar and for some reason I felt extremely embarrassed. He didn't recognize me, or perhaps he was embarrassed himself.

But this was an isolated case; it didn't make us stop trusting our friends.

With Papa away, life on the kolkhoz grew harder and harder. When Mama was sick with malaria, I had to do everything on my own. In the morning before leaving for school, I had to clean out the pigsty and then feed the pigs, carrying the heavy buckets of water and feed. It was gruelling work for a child of twelve, and by the time I got to school I was exhausted. Every other day, I had to go pick up our bread ration at the administrative depot, several kilometres away on the other side of town. On the way back home, it was all I could do to keep from taking a bite from one of the round white loaves.

Getting fuel for our stoves, in the house and in the pigsty, was also a major task. I would gather wood from wherever I could find it — occasionally, I even pulled off a piece of fence or railing. I didn't feel in the least guilty about this, only afraid of being caught. Our main fuel, however, was *kiziak,* which was made from horse or cow manure and a bit of straw. We kneaded the mixture into flat cakes which were then stuck to the wall. Once they had dried, they fell to the floor. Another of my chores was to pick up cow patties and horse droppings from the street. Many children had to do this. It wasn't very pleasant work, but at least the horse dung was dryer and didn't stain your hands ...

Mama knew that we couldn't go on living like this. In town, there was less to eat for refugees, but they didn't do too badly. Our closest friends, the Brums, a Polish-Jewish couple, persuaded Mama to leave the kolkhoz for a less tiring job in town. A job came up quite soon, that of bookkeeper in an orphanage. Mama didn't know the first thing about bookkeeping, but Mr. Brum, a bookkeeper himself, promised to give her a few lessons and to help her whenever she needed it.

Chapter 12

AFTER SOME HESITATION, we decided to leave the kolkhoz, where we had lived for sixteen long months. I was sad to leave my little piglets behind, but the prospect of having less work, living closer to school and being able to spend more time with my friends quickly cheered me up.

This time the move was more difficult, since we had acquired so much, including the chickens, a lamb that we had bought for its wool, a sack of rice and the vegetables from our kitchen garden. We rented a cart, and with the lamb and chickens walking behind us, set out, making sure not to lose any of the possessions we had worked so hard for. It was a very tiring trip for us, but the little procession was probably a comical sight for anyone watching. This time, I didn't care. Usually so sensitive to ridicule and always careful to not stand out, I was too happy to be leaving the kolkhoz and beginning a new life to care about the Uzbeks' jeers.

We rented a little storeroom in the home of an Uzbek family, the Shamdamovs, whom Mama had met when she worked at the institute for blind children. This room had been a sheepfold, as we were constantly reminded by the lingering smell. Since the roof was quite damaged, it would be liveable only until the rainy season began. Our daily life took place mainly in the courtyard surrounded by high clay walls. That is where we ate, cooked, and washed — both ourselves and the laundry. During the summer the Shamdamovs slept in the courtyard, on a wooden platform covered with mosquito netting. Now I could see more of Uzbek daily life. I saw, for example, that the women washed their hair with curdled milk, which made it beautifully shiny. After rinsing several times, they would plait their hair into lots of little braids, and then they wouldn't touch it for a month.

Uzbeks had the custom of sleeping in the same clothes that they wore in the daytime. When their clothes got dirty, they changed, and again wore the same outfit night and day. We did our best not to sleep in our daytime clothes. I can imagine how amazed the Shamdamovs must have been to see us changing in and out of our rags so often. Our hosts were religious and Mr. Shamdamov said his prayers two or three times a day. They also observed Ramadan, the most important holiday. It lasted a month, during which they fasted until sundown. But then they had a veritable feast, to which they invited friends and relations. We benefited from their generous hospitality, as they sometimes invited us to their Ramadan supper. The main dish was pilaf, made with lamb, rice, and vegetables, well-seasoned and quite greasy. We ate by dipping our fingers into a big bowl which was passed around the table.

I learned how baking was done in the big, tall-footed clay bread oven found in every Uzbek courtyard. A wood fire was lit and when the oven was hot enough, flat, round loaves were stuck against the oven walls. The bakers wore thick mitts so they wouldn't burn their hands. When the loaves were ready, they fell off. The process reminded me of how we made *kiziak,* the manure cakes, but this didn't spoil my appetite.

Little by little the last reminders of our country life disappeared. Our lamb broke its foot one day when it was frightened by the Shamdamovs' son, and then it began to lose its appetite. Mr. Shamdamov bought it from us and the lamb miraculously recovered after a few days. We also got rid of the chickens. Life became much simpler. We had enough to eat, with the produce we had brought from the kolkhoz and our bread ration. Mama ate her meals at the orphanage, which left more food for me.

I was still unhappy about my wardrobe. I judged myself the worst-dressed girl in the class. My dream was to own high leather boots and a goat-hair shawl. I considered these crocheted shawls the height of elegance. They were also good protection from the winter damp and cold. Several of the girls had them and I envied them greatly. But for all the time we were in the Soviet Union, I never managed to buy one — not even in Moscow, where the winters were really harsh.

We were still very poor, but we had a bit more clothing. Sometimes when I looked in a mirror, I told myself that I didn't really look that bad. Those brief moments gave me the confidence that every girl needs so much at that age.

And yet, I had little reason to feel good about myself. I was alone with my mother, uprooted, in a foreign country in the middle of nowhere, with my father so far away ... enough to make anyone feel lost!

When the rainy season arrived, the question of our lodging arose again. The Shamdamovs invited us inside their house to warm up a bit, but even there it was very cold. There was no stove and, as was typical of Uzbek houses, the only source of heat was a hole filled with embers in the middle of the room. We sat around a low table placed over this fireplace and slipped our feet under a big blanket covering the table. It wasn't great, but it was better than our little shed, which had nothing.

So it was urgent to find other lodgings for the winter.

In the house next door lived a Russian family, the Budiakovs — the father, the mother, Niura, a girl of sixteen, and her seventeen-year-old brother Sasha. The Budiakovs' two older sons were at the front. They were typical of Russian families in Uzbekistan. As with other Russian or Ukrainian families, we didn't know where they were from, or when and why they had come to Uzbekistan. No one would dream of asking; we acted as if they had always been there. Much later I learned that all of these displaced families were victims of Stalin's purges and had been deported for reasons that were unknown often even to them. They kept quiet, grateful that they hadn't been shot. At that time, I knew nothing of the Stalinist purges and deportations. In fact, I was certain that the Soviet system was the best, and I was convinced of the great wisdom and even greater goodness of Papa Joe Stalin. That was how he was described at school and on the radio; that was what was written in the newspapers and in most of the books we read.

The Budiakovs' house consisted of a bedroom and a large kitchen. To make ends meet, they agreed to rent us the bedroom.

Mr. Budiakov worked in a cottonseed-oil factory, where huge presses extracted oil from cotton seeds, producing cakes of a yellow substance called *zhmikh,* which was used as animal feed. Although it was supposed to be unfit for human consumption, we had eaten *zhmikh* during the worst of the famine when we first came to Uzbekistan. Workers' wages were pathetic and it was hard to support a family on so little. Mr. Budiakov got ration tickets for 600 grams of bread per day, but most of his income came from theft. Like most of the other workers, he left the factory almost every day with a small bottle of oil hidden under his clothes. There was no oil in the shops and it was easy to find takers willing to pay a very good price. These buyers were themselves stealing other items from their own workplace, which they would sell to get cash, and so it went. During the war, there was no other way to survive. This trafficking was discussed openly, unlike politics and the regime. No one considered such thieving to be a real crime and no one worried about being denounced. After all, it was only stealing from the State ...

The Budiakovs had other sources of income. Their son Sasha worked in a shoemakers' co-operative. I don't know whether he stole it or just bought it a reduced price, but he would bring home leather and make shoes and boots, which he sold at the Sunday market. That is how I finally wound up with the leather boots that I had longed for.

Mrs. Budiakov worked as a cleaning lady in a school, for the sole purpose of obtaining bread tickets. Niura helped her, and when they were done they came home to their main job: spinning wool and knitting gloves, socks and sweaters to sell at the Sunday market. This work filled their evenings. Often Niura's friends would come over. By the light of an oil lamp, everyone was kept busy — the mother spinning the wool (for that was the most difficult task and even Niura wasn't very good at it), Sasha making boots and the girls knitting. Their hands flew and it didn't take long for the garments to take shape.

The friend who came most often was Marusia, a tall girl with blond braids wound around her head. She was secretly in love with Sasha. While they worked, the girls sang old Russian and Ukrainian folk songs or patriotic songs celebrating the faithfulness of the women awaiting the triumphant return of their husbands or fiancés. The best singer was Marusia. It was a pleasure to listen to her high voice, strong and pure, filling the room.

Niura didn't go to school. She thought it wasn't worth the effort: it was better to earn as much money as possible and enjoy life. She was a stocky girl, not very pretty but comfortable with herself. She had dark brown hair, twisted with ribbons into two braids wound around a wide, pale face with regular features and no distinguishing traits.

Under her bed she kept a little suitcase, which no one was allowed to touch. In it were her treasures: a skirt of navy blue satin (always carefully pressed), a white silk blouse, a pair of well-polished black shoes, two pairs of white socks with blue stripes, a few embroidered handkerchiefs, a little mirror, a leather handbag, a few photos and a large notebook containing the words to several songs that she and her friends had copied out. Each girl had a notebook in which her friends would write song lyrics or a poem, or make a drawing. Nearly every day, Niura would open her suitcase to gaze at her treasures, making sure that everything was there and all was in order. At these moments, she felt rich and confident about life.

Once or twice a week, she would go out with a group of friends. On Sundays, they went to the cinema; the other days, they went for walks or spent the evening at one of the girls' houses. I didn't know them, because they never came to Niura's house. Little by little, she began to tell me things. She told me that she had a Gypsy boyfriend; she could no longer see him because he was in prison, but they would be together again when he got out. She didn't tell me what he had done to be sent to prison. But several times she made me swear to keep all this a secret. She probably didn't want her parents to know, since they were very strict when it came to their daughter's virtue. I have to admit that I didn't really understand the secrecy. Although I had read a few books that talked about love, I was too young to grasp why a girl's virtue was a matter of such importance.

Even though Niura was quite a bit older than me and I was very naive for my age, she still befriended me and was fond of me. Perhaps she felt sorry for me, in my loneliness. I had no lover, no friends, and I never went to the cinema. My life must have seemed dreary and monotonous to her, and she wasn't far from the truth. She decided to make me part of her group and to invite me on their outings.

Niura's friends were not, strictly speaking, *ogoltsi,* but they knew *ogoltsi.* Even though they didn't go to school or work, they often had large sums of money from mysterious sources. But they were kind and jolly, and I was happy to be included. I went out more and more often and came home later and later. My mother wasn't pleased, but I ignored her. It was more important to me to win the trust and friendship of my new companions than to please my mother.

Niura and I did nothing wrong, but I am certain now that eventually we would have been led into trouble. Some of my new friends lived a far from blameless life. There were two Gypsy girls, for example, who would often tell us of the guys they went out with just for the stuff they could get from them. Boys would appear suddenly with large sums of money that they would spend blithely on food, drink, and cigarettes. I didn't ask any questions. I happily ate what was offered, but I never smoked or drank.

There were all sorts of stories told within the group. Stories about one of their heroes, Grisza, who was serving a long prison term for killing a policeman; or about a girl who had been raped by guys who had been sent by other girls to take revenge. I heard all kinds of other anecdotes which were considered to be just as "amusing". Grisza killed a policeman? Good for him, as long as he gets out of prison soon. A girl was raped? She probably deserved it. How did I react, the good little mama's girl, so sweet and naive? I didn't judge them harshly. They fascinated me. They were so sure of themselves, so grownup and independent. When I was with them, I felt stronger and braver. I no longer had to be afraid people would throw stones at me and insult me. I had a new feeling of belonging, and it made me feel safe.

The relationships between boys and girls in this group were similar to those I had seen at school: a boy would ask a girl to go steady, and the only way she could refuse was if she already had a boyfriend. It was absolutely inconceivable to say, "No, I don't like you," which would have been the supreme insult. Quite soon, a boy popped the question to me and since of course I was unattached, I had to accept. I didn't have the slightest idea what this relationship might involve. I had seen boys and girls holding hands at the cinema, and suspected they also kissed, but that was all. I didn't know what else there might be.

This boy's name was Boris. He was a tall blond boy, with an ordinary face covered with freckles. He was quiet and always smiling. So I said "yes," and we began to go out together. We would hold hands and kiss each other on the cheek, and I liked it. I was happy to have my own boyfriend, someone who would wait for me and was happy to see me. But quickly the kisses on the cheek turned into kisses on the mouth, and I liked that a lot less. I had been told so often that it wasn't healthy to eat from the same spoon as anyone else or drink from the same glass. I had completely forgotten the old "tongue to tongue" games of my childhood, which hadn't seemed so unpleasant at the time. I put up with the kisses on the mouth, remaining totally passive, of course. When Boris began to fondle my budding breasts, I found it degrading and I broke up with him. He immediately started going out with another girl, and I had to accept this gracefully.

Shortly afterwards, another boy asked me if I wanted to be his girlfriend. He was a Korean boy named Moses Ten, nicknamed Mossia. (There were a lot of Koreans in Namangan, and most of them had the last name of Kim, Ten, or Li.) I accepted, because I couldn't think up a good reason for refusing. I liked Mossia better than Boris, because he was gentler and seemed charmed with me. He gave me little presents, including a postcard with a photo of Pushkin's wife, a very lovely and elegant woman. I kept this card for several years, although now I'm not quite sure why. But sure enough, our relationship followed the same old pattern: kisses on the cheek, then kisses on the mouth, followed by the fondling I found so degrading and vulgar. No, I was definitely not ready for this kind of relationship yet.

In short, I broke up with Mossia too after a few weeks, and that was the end of my experiences with boyfriends for quite a while.

In the meantime, Papa had returned from the Urals, and my parents began to think once more about my education. They didn't approve of my mysterious night-time outings, or my coarse language. And worst of all, friends of my parents had seen me with a group of boys and girls who were rudely stopping passersby and demanding cigarettes.

Chapter 13

AFTER CONSULTING A few friends, my parents decided to put me in the Polish orphanage which had just opened. This decision made me very unhappy. I felt deeply ashamed to be in an orphanage when both my parents were alive. But the only alternative would have been to run away from home, and I wasn't about to do that. I'd known a few girls who had run away. I still remember one: Nina, the daughter of a doctor in Kharkov. We had been in the same class for a while, and when we lived at the kolkhoz, she and I would sometimes walk home from school together. She was a pretty girl, with curly blond hair and big blue eyes. She always complained of being cold and hungry at home, and she was fed up with her miserable life and with school. She dropped out of school and broke off all contact with her family. I, too, lost touch with her. There were rumours that she was hanging out with a gang of *ogoltsi,* that she was parading around town, dressed to the nines and looking very alluring. Just before I left Namangan, I heard that Nina had been in serious trouble and had spent some time in prison. Even children from good families sometimes quit school, took up with hoodlums and began to lead a life of crime.

I was less of a rebel myself — or perhaps I just didn't have the nerve, although I had no moral scruples about running away. At that age, you easily take on the morals of your peers over those you were raised with.

The Polish orphanage in Namangan had opened at the same time as the delegations of the Polish government in exile appeared. Famine and disease had left many children orphans, and it was important to find them so they wouldn't be placed in Soviet orphanages, where conditions were very bad and the children would lose their Polish identity.

There were about a hundred children in our orphanage, from three to sixteen years old, who had lost one or both of their parents. After the age of sixteen, you were supposed to leave the orphanage and make your own way, but some stayed on a bit longer, for various reasons: two of the boys were finishing their apprenticeships, and a seriously handicapped girl stayed to help out with the younger children. Most of the children went to the Russian school, but we also had classes in Polish history and literature in the orphanage, and we were taught Polish songs and dances — the *krakoviak* and the *kujawiak*. We put on shows and invited parents and Polish friends.

All of the children except the very youngest helped with the housework. We had a number of chores, some more enjoyable than others. One week the assignment would be to help out in the kitchen, which we liked a lot, since we got an extra bowl of soup. The next it would be helping out in the dormitories, which was much harder. The job everyone liked the most was bread duty: it meant waking very early in the morning to go into town to get the bread ration for everyone. You had to carry heavy sacks on your back, but your reward was an extra piece of bread.

I quickly came to love life at the orphanage, especially the teachers and my new comrades. They were very different from Niura, and a better fit with the values I had been raised with. I couldn't understand how I could have hung out with that gang of punks. In the orphanage, children and adults came from Catholic or Jewish families, but this difference didn't cause problems. Many of the boarders came from well-educated Polish families, so we read lots of books and discussed them. We also had more earthy conversations: the older girls would inform the younger ones on matters of sex, and I finally found out about menstruation and that mysterious virtue that had to be defended at any cost and kept intact until marriage.

It was at the orphanage that I realized how nice it would have been not to be an only child. Some children had brothers and sisters at the orphanage. The older girls looked after the younger children, protecting them and making sure they were well-fed and properly dressed. The thirteen- and fourteen-year-old girls knit clothing that they sold outside the orphanage. With the money they earned, they bought food for themselves and their siblings. This was much needed: there was never enough food at the orphanage, and what there was wasn't very good. The little children with older brothers or sisters felt more secure and didn't miss their parents, who had died or were in prison, so badly.

We had other pastimes that were less innocent than knitting. We would organize expeditions to steal fruit from Uzbeks. Often we had to run for our lives to escape from the owners, who would sometimes chase after us brandishing a hatchet. It was very exciting, and it made up for the lack of sports! We had several ways to go about these raids. The simplest was to jump over the orchard fence, pick up the fruit as fast as we could and jump back over the fence. Another was to go to the Uzbeks' stands, supposedly to buy fruit. While one person bargained with the owner, the others would sneak handfuls of fruit from the baskets. This method was more dangerous, for if we'd been caught it would have been difficult to escape. And it required a bit of money, which we rarely had. The third strategy was carried out in the market. The boys would harass the sellers by crying *"Urtak, nishpul kutak?"* which means "Comrade, how much for your dickie?", and the girls would snatch fruit from the stands in the ensuing uproar.

Despite all this, I didn't manage to make any real friends among the girls in the orphanage. But at the Russian school I became friends again with Lena Prokofieva, although we had grown apart during the time I hung around with Niura's gang. Lena and I, along with Zina and Liza, soon formed an inseparable foursome.

As soon as my parents could be sure that Niura and her gang were a thing of the past, they took me out of the orphanage. Perhaps they felt guilty about taking a place from a genuine orphan. To be on the safe side, they also decided to move, using the excuse that there wasn't enough room for us at the Budiakovs'.

We moved to our fifth home in Namangan — once again, a small dark room, with a tiny window and a dirt floor. It was in a typical clay Uzbek house, one of a group of cabins surrounding a central courtyard where people lived much of their lives in full view of the neighbours. Quarrels and shouting were part of everyday life, especially since there were quite a few "loose" women who were seen every day in the company of a different man. My parents thought that while this might have been interesting for me, it wasn't very educational, and they quickly decided to find another place to live.

One of my chores at home was the laundry, which was done in the courtyard. Soap was scarce, so I would rub our rags with wood ash and then rinse them several times. Then I would hang them on a clothesline in the courtyard. One of my favourite possessions — a plaid skirt that I'd had since Wilno and which I hardly ever wore so it wouldn't wear out — disappeared one day from the clothesline. Then a red woollen dress that I had been given at the orphanage went missing. I was wretched at losing the only two pretty things I owned. Not long afterwards at the market, Papa and I spotted a woman who was selling an ugly dress made from my two stolen treasures. But we didn't dare confront her.

Like everyone else, we did our cooking in the courtyard, in a pot set on two bricks. I still had to gather wood for the fire and manure to make *kiziak*. Matches were as scarce as soap, so we would generally ask the neighbours for a few coals to start our fire.

My father had found a job as inspector at the Ministry of Education. He would visit schools and orphanages to audit their books. He was always depressed when he returned home. Everywhere, he was offered bribes, which he immediately refused. Word spread quickly that this new inspector could not be bought, even though all his colleagues were involved in deals and skimmed off their share of the loot. There was theft everywhere. Papa was supposed to report any irregularities, but that would be leaving himself open to revenge. A knife in the back in some dark alleyway could come at any time.

The situation was impossible. My father was no rebel; he had no ambition to change the way of the world. He was simply a very honest man, and he couldn't bear the constant offers of bribes. His solution was to turn a blind eye to irregularities, if the children in the school or orphanage seemed happy and healthy. On the other hand, if the children looked emaciated and sad, he would do a strict audit and submit a report. In the first situation, he would even reluctantly accept gifts. Everyone did the same thing. That was what life was like in the great and powerful Soviet Union. But Papa was not comfortable with it. My parents fretted over the situation constantly and tried to find a way out. I could hear them whispering late into the night.

Much later, when we had returned to Poland, I found out what was in fact the main cause of their worry. My father had been summoned by the secret police, the

NKVD*, who wanted him to become an informer. First he was left in a waiting room to stew for several hours, then an officer took him into his office and explained what he could do for his "new country" by reporting the conversations of his friends. Some of Papa's friends did indeed belong to the Bund, a social-democratic Jewish organization, which, in the Soviet Union, was a crime punishable by prison or internment in a labour camp. Like his Bundist friends, my father was opposed to the Soviet regime, but he never actually acted against it. It was all just talk. My mother, as I have said, had been attracted to communism before the war, but our stay in Uzbekistan had cured her of her illusions.

My father refused to collaborate with the police. He said that he would be willing, but it would never work. His friends would see immediately from his face that something was up. The officer told him that anyone could do it and not to forget Siberia. My father replied that you can live in Siberia like anywhere else; there were plenty of people living in Siberia. The NKVD officers finally let him go, after making him sign a paper promising that he would repeat this conversation to no one, not even his wife. They warned him that he would be summoned again, and told him he would be well advised to think it over. He never was summoned again, but the threat was always there.

So my parents began to think about leaving Namangan. This was no easy matter. Without a *laissez-passer*, a pass issued by the authorities, you couldn't go anywhere or

* an early acronym for the secret police, which later became widely known as the KGB.

even buy a train ticket. To rent an apartment you had to have a residence permit. It had to be filed at the police station within twenty-four hours of arrival, otherwise your status was flagrantly illegal.

My father had briefly considered joining the Polish army that was then forming in Soviet territory under General Anders, following a treaty between Stalin and the Polish government in exile. The mobilization centres were in Central Asia and, according to the rumours, the Army was being sent to Iran and Pakistan. Apart from the desire to fight against the Germans, there was also the wish to get out of the Soviet Union. For my father, however, this was really not feasible. He had never done his military service and he was nearly fifty years old, no longer of an age to fight. On top of that, people said that Jews were not welcome.

My friendship with Lena, Zina, and Liza grew stronger. We were inseparable. Not a day went by that we didn't meet after school to go see a film or take a walk in town. We talked of everything: books we were reading, life, the future. All four of us intended to join the Comsomol, the communist youth group, and we had no doubts about the superiority of the communist system and the Soviet Union. However, we were much more interested in boys and love than in politics. In this, we were no different from girls our age living in a capitalist country. We read a lot, mainly Russian authors, but also whatever foreign authors were allowed, like Stefan Zweig, Guy de Maupassant and Thomas Mann.

In the spring, we decided to take an excursion to the countryside. I had never been out of the town, and the idea excited me. In Namangan, there was no point in going out to the country in the summertime, since all the vegetation was dried out and burned by the sun. In the winter it rained constantly and there was nothing but mud. The only enjoyable season for an outing was the springtime, when plants covered the hills and little flowers, called *gulbara,* made a yellow-and-green mosaic on the ground. We'd heard it was a splendid sight.

So we six girls set off on our excursion, Wiera and Tata having joined our usual foursome. Wiera was a little blond girl, with an ordinary face. Tata, however, was special. She was tall and robust; people called her *ochayannaya,* which means "bold and wild". She loved a good fight and was afraid of nothing and no one; the boys in our class preferred to keep out of her way.

We were walking along, picking flowers and chatting when, at a bend in the road, we saw a group of boys playing ball. There were eight of them. We knew two: an Uzbek boy a few years older than us, who often threw stones at me and called me names on the way home from school; and a second boy who had been in our class at school, before he dropped out and supposedly joined a gang of *ogoltsi.* The boys started out by taunting us with rude names and then tried to surround us, but we managed to escape by running off into the hills. Once we were safe, we stopped to try and figure out what to do. How could we get back to town? There was only one road. We could try to cut across the hills, but they all looked alike and we could easily get lost. We decided that our only chance was to stay together. None of us should run off, for the boys would only catch her.

What we feared was exactly what happened. The boys were waiting for us at the side of the road. Wiera and I were walking together side by side. They started out on Wiera, pulling her braids and pinching her here and there. She couldn't bear it and ran off as fast as she could. They didn't try to catch her, but turned on me instead. To my great shame, I did just as Wiera had done, running away as fast as I could. This time, they gave chase and caught me. Excited by their fun, they threw me on the ground and started pulling my clothes off. I fought like a mother lion, but they were much stronger and there were so many of them! I had no hope of escaping and was in a total panic. As they were about to take off my underpants, the other girls came running to my rescue. Little Lena threw herself at the biggest boy, the Uzbek, and standing on her tiptoes, gave him a resounding slap. Then big Tata arrived, hitting out in all directions with her shoe. I got up and joined the fray. Only Wiera stood off at a distance, watching.

We emerged from the fight battered and bruised, but the boys had fled. I was so ashamed of my cowardice in running away that for several years I thought of it as the most disgraceful episode of my life. But I never forget how solidarity and true friendship had saved the day.

Chapter 14

MY PARENTS WERE DOING all they could to get out of Namangan and go to Moscow. They corresponded back and forth with some useful contacts, including a cousin of my father's, a well-known Communist who at the time held an important position in the Union of Polish Patriots, an organization created by the Soviet government and Polish communists and sympathizers, with the aim of taking power in Poland after it was liberated.

This cousin had promised Papa that he would arrange for our move. Mama had helped the communists before the war, and that worked in our favour. We finally got the go-ahead. My parents were very happy, but I wasn't. I had close friends, especially Lena, whom I loved and admired and shared everything with. I liked my class at school and our teacher. For the first time in my life, I was happy with myself and my situation, and I didn't want to leave it all behind. If someone had suggested then that I should stay in Uzbekistan for the rest of my days, I would have agreed without a second thought. Fortunately, no one paid any attention to my opinion.

There was another reason for my happiness in Namangan. We had found another apartment, with a wooden floor and a real Russian stove. The four of us — Lena, Zina, Liza, and I — had cleaned the whole place thoroughly, from floor to ceiling. I had been so happy! But like it or not, I had to accept reality.

We began to prepare for our move. There were many formalities to take care of. Packing was easy, since we had practically nothing. Saying farewell to my friends, however, was very sad. The four of us cried and vowed we would never forget one another. Lena and I promised solemnly to write to one another for the rest of our lives. To my great surprise, the principal of the school, when he learned I was leaving, allowed Lena, Zina, and Liza to miss classes so they could come to the station and see me off. How astonished I was when I saw the principal had come too! I was genuinely touched. Not only did he think it important to come, but he also gave a speech on the value of friendship. He was a strict teacher and all the students were afraid of him, but suddenly I saw him in a new light and I liked him much more.

The train pulled out of the station; an important, difficult stage in my life had come to an end.

Lena and I wrote to each other for four years. The last letter she sent was from Tashkent, where she had enrolled in university. But then the letters stopped. I don't think that she forgot me. It might have been that she ran into problems for corresponding with a foreigner. There could have been any number of reasons. People of independent character like her, too strong-minded and too honest, could wind up in prison or a work camp for a single casual remark.

I remember little about the journey to Moscow. My thoughts were more on what I was leaving behind than what awaited me. I had another bout of malaria, fortunately my last. On the trip I talked a lot with a young soldier who had been demobilized and was going home. He was a good-looking boy and I was pleased at his attentions. Then, all at once, he was seized by convulsions. It looked like an epileptic seizure, caused by a war wound. All the passengers felt tremendous sympathy for this boy, so young and so handsome. There was an old woman who looked after him tenderly. She called him "Rose Flower" and nicknamed me "Flower Bud".

In this friendly atmosphere, the trip passed quickly and soon we were in Moscow. We were put up in a large hotel, the Severnaja, quite a way from downtown. It was nothing like modern hotels. Most of the rooms were dormitories with ten to twenty beds in each. On the upper floors, there were a few smaller rooms, but they were all occupied. We were put in a room with thirteen other people, including four couples, all of them Polish. The beds were arranged with the head against the wall and the foot towards the middle of the room, with night tables in between. People whispered that one of the couples — a tall blonde woman and an old bearded man — was not even married. They had made a little private space for themselves, using a blanket for a curtain. They must have thought that no one could hear them. Every night strange noises came from behind the curtain, and before long the inevitable happened: their curtain-wall collapsed and there they were, stark naked in a welter of blankets and pillows! There was a great commotion and everyone had a good laugh.

Another occupant of the room was very intriguing to me. This was a woman, a philosophy professor (she was to become famous after the war), who spent her days in bed. She kept a pot of boiled potatoes under the bed, and every two or three minutes she would spear one and greedily devour it.

This new environment was strange, but it didn't really faze me. I was now quite different from the spoiled little girl I'd been before the war. I had lived through so much that nothing surprised me anymore, although I was still very naive and ignorant about certain things. For example, during the summer vacation, I would sometimes lie on my bed quietly reading, with no one else in the room but a young couple. I couldn't understand why they kept suggesting so insistently that I go outside, to a movie or something. They said it was very bad for my health to stay inside all day long, that I really should get some fresh air and exercise. I was astonished that they were so concerned about my health, but remained stubbornly on my bed. One time I did give in, but I came back right away because I had forgotten something. I found the door locked and I knocked in vain for a quite a while before it finally dawned on me ...

A long spell of boredom set in. I spent a lot of time at home, because I hadn't made any friends yet in Moscow and I didn't have anywhere to go. Despite our lack of privacy, we were grateful that we no longer had to live as we had in Namangan. Both my parents had work as bookkeepers, Papa at the Union of Patriots and Mama at the Polish Radio. They earned much more money than in Uzbekistan, and we had access to a special store where we could buy things that we had almost forgotten existed. Our daily life was far better: We had butter, cheese, sausage, and candy, even chocolate. I hadn't seen chocolate for years and I ate incredible amounts.

That was how the Soviet government bought the allegiance of its future collaborators. Our special store was at the lowest rung of this system. The privileges you could enjoy depended on the position you held. The political leaders of the Union of Patriots could go to other stores with even better stocks. As for the Soviet leaders, who can say? This all took place in secret, and I never saw another store but the one we were allowed to use.

The period of hunger was behind us, but it wasn't all for the best. I had gained a few kilos and now I was once again too plump. I didn't like this, although it was not unusual among girls my age. After all those years of hunger, I was incapable of holding myself back.

I was now in Grade 8 and couldn't afford to be out of school for too long. My parents enrolled me in a girls' school, since it had a good reputation and several Polish girls went there, so I could make friends and get any help I needed with my studies. The level of instruction in Moscow was much higher than it had been in Namangan.

One of the girls in my class was the daughter of well-known Polish Communists. I was taken to her house to meet her, so I wouldn't feel so lost at my new school. This girl treated me with icy coldness. She looked down her nose at me and said not a word. Nor did her attitude change in the days to come. Instead of offering comfort, she only made me feel sadder and lonelier.

Later, I wondered about this situation. Why did Polish Communists, most of whom were Jewish, show such scorn for those who weren't one of them? You'd think that in their struggle for the good of humanity, they might have felt a bit of sympathy for the disadvantaged. Instead, they acted like the chosen people, more intelligent and more important than ordinary folk. In fact, they were preparing themselves for their future role in the government. Later on, when I became a member of the Polish youth organization in Poland, I met with the same disdain. I was always considered a bit of an outsider, for reasons I could never fathom.

So I began at my girls' school, which was quite different from the school at Namangan. It was a normal school — that is, discipline was strict and the teachers were demanding. You had to work hard to earn good grades. The girls were very sure of themselves and much better dressed than at Namangan. They already wore makeup, but very discreetly, as makeup wasn't allowed at school. Some of them went out with boys, and this was the main topic of their conversations. But they also talked about the new films, actors, performances at the Bolshoi Ballet, books ...

Even during the war, Moscow had a flourishing cultural scene, with a wide choice of entertainment: concerts, theatre, ballet, opera. For a little provincial girl like me, this was all completely new. I had never been to the theatre before, I knew nothing about music, and I didn't even have a crush on an actor. So I was of no interest to the girls in my class. They were nice to me, but no more. In the winter, I went skating with one of them a few times and we did our homework together, but it was a far cry from the friendship that I longed for.

I joined the literary club where, after class, the members would discuss books we had read. I enjoyed these meetings, although I was too timid to speak. I was happy enough to listen to the others. I worked conscientiously at home and was attentive in class. I got high marks for my compositions on Russian literature and good grades in the other subjects as well. This was probably because I had no friends, and all my time was devoted to study and reading.

A few months after the school year began, a new girl, named Irena, came to our class. Her father, like mine, was a Polish Jew who worked for the Union of Patriots, so we soon became acquainted. He was a communist who had fled their home town, Lvov, when the Germans invaded. Like us, he had wound up somewhere in the Soviet Union, but his wife and daughter had stayed in Lvov, confined to the ghetto. When it became clear what fate awaited the Jews, Irena's mother sent her to be sheltered with a Polish family. It was just for a day or two, she said, while she went back to the ghetto to get their things together to leave. She never came back. In a massive raid on the Lvov ghetto, the Nazis killed thousands of Jews. Irena's mother was probably one of them.

Irena stayed with the Polish family, a mother and daughter. They weren't happy risking their lives for a virtual stranger, but as good Christians, they were not about to condemn another human being to certain death either. Irena spent fourteen months with them, half of the time hidden under a bed. A German was staying in the next room. Only after he left could Irena come out of hiding, and even then she couldn't move freely in the apartment in case the neighbours should see her. The rest of the time she spent hidden in the bathroom. These fourteen months in hiding almost drove her mad. After the Russians liberated Lvov, her father tracked her down and had her come to Moscow. And that is how Irena entered my life. Very quickly a friendship formed between us that has lasted to this day.

Irena and her father lived in a large apartment where several Polish families were all crowded together. Each family had a bedroom, and they shared the kitchen and a large common room. All the Poles in Moscow were familiar with this type of apartment, because they either lived in one or had visited friends who did. Daily life was difficult and disputes were frequent, especially in the shared kitchen. Some people would take others' pots right off the fire and put on their own. Once, a woman spat in the soup pot of another who, maddened with rage, picked up the pot and poured the soup over her flatmate's head.

Irena's father was expecting his life to be a little easier now that he had his daughter to look after the household, but he had a rude awakening. Irena did not know how to cook and had no interest in housework. They quarrelled. The truth was, Irena didn't like her father, a dislike she'd felt since infancy, and their relationship worsened daily. Irena and I grew very close, although our personalities were quite different. What brought us together was probably our shared language and background, and similar childhood memories. And more important, we shared a feeling of isolation in a foreign environment where it was difficult to fit in. Our relationships with the other girls were superficial and never came close to being the kind of friendship we longed for.

Irena and I both loved cultural outings. We began to go often to the cinema and the theatre. We went a few times to the famous Bolshoi Ballet of Moscow. I remember in particular two dazzling performances of *Swan Lake* and *Scheherazade*. There were several theatres in Moscow and tickets sold out well in advance. Just before the performances, scalpers would offer them at inflated prices. Even though we rarely had much money, Irena and I would go to see a play whenever we could.

We also took long walks across the city, in the parks and cemeteries and along the Moscow River. Sometimes a few boys would join us, the sons of Union of Patriots employees. They were just friends, but Irena liked to pretend they were all in love with her. She often asked me how many boys had declared their love to me. I would admit, shamefully, that this had never happened, while she would claim that she had already received several offers of marriage. I doubted this, but I still felt devastated that no one desired me so much. I was very shy and I felt ugly and fat beside Irena, who was radiant and confident in her powers of seduction. Despite all this, we were still great friends.

Moscow was the first big city I had lived in. Before the war, I had been taken to Warsaw only a few times, and I could scarcely remember Wilno. I delighted in discovering Moscow, the museums, the Tretiakov gallery, and of course, Lenin's tomb! There was always a long line of people waiting to visit the tomb, looking as downcast as if Lenin had died only the day before. It was like being at a funeral. I remember that when the time came for me to walk past the open casket where Lenin's body lay, I was suddenly seized by an irresistible desire to laugh. I stifled it as best I could, but a snicker escaped, to the indignation of all the people around me. They told me off severely and I felt terrible, like a criminal.

Chapter 15

THE END OF THE WAR AT LAST! It was a celebration I have never forgotten. May 9, 1945, only a few weeks after our arrival in Moscow. A jubilant crowd filled the streets. There were fireworks — the first I'd ever seen — and music, and happy people laughing, drinking, singing and kissing one another. There was a general feeling of camaraderie in the streets. The hellish war had finally ended, and those who had survived could now live in peace and happiness. That is what everyone hoped. The Russians were to learn soon enough that such happiness was not the fate of all. The personality cult of Stalin was prevalent at that time in the Soviet Union. Stalin was represented as a kind-hearted old father figure; in reality, he was a suspicious and cruel man, who saw everyone as a potential traitor. Especially suspect were people who had had contact with the non-communist world, even those who had been prisoners of war and had been persecuted in the most terrible concentration camps.

Very quickly there came a wave of arrests and deportations. All the former prisoners of war were affected, everyone who had been living under the German occupation or held in the Nazi camps. In the eyes of the regime, they were all suspect. For this devastated country and its inhabitants worn down by the years of war, a new tragedy was unfolding.

We began to receive horrifying reports from liberated Poland. At the time, we had some idea of what the Germans had done to the Polish people, especially those of Jewish background. But people just could not grasp the full extent of this tragedy, and we all continued to hope for news of our families and friends. It was unconceivable that the vast majority of them had died at the hands of the Germans, such a great and civilized people. In the first half of 1945, Polish exiles began to return to liberated Poland. The news they sent back grew more and more horrific. Rarely would anyone learn that a family member had survived. Even in the face of indisputable evidence, people kept on hoping, kept on waiting still.

My mother's immediate family was wiped out. My beloved Aunt Zosia, my Uncle Simon and his wife and two children, Ala and Bronek, had all disappeared. Someone had seen Ala, dying, on a street in the ghetto. The others had probably perished in the gas chambers at Treblinka. There was no witness who could tell of their last hours.

Aunt Zosia had spent part of the German occupation at Rodosc, near Miedzeszyn. She had managed to get false identity papers — "Aryan papers" — and had rented a room in a little house. Since she had no money, she had given shelter to a Jewish couple who were better off and could support her. Someone denounced them, and the Germans came and shot the man and the woman. My aunt, who was not suspected of being Jewish but merely of having sheltered Jews, might have been spared had she not, distraught, begun to shout, "I'm Jewish too! You've massacred my whole family, you've killed them all. Kill me too, kill me!"

Which they lost no time in doing, then and there. The owner of the house where Aunt Zosia had rented her room told this story to my father.

Two cousins of my mother's had died in the Hôtel Polonais. They had been lured there by the Germans, who promised that Jews who held a visa to go abroad could live in the hotel until their departure date. Instead, most were sent to concentration camps. Mama never learned how her other aunts, uncles and cousins died.

Only one of my mother's uncles survived — the one we had stayed with in Bialystok, in 1939, on the way to Wilno. The Russians had deported him to Siberia. All the others died in the Bialystok ghetto.

My father's family was more assimilated into mainstream Polish society. They had contacts outside the ghetto, which gave them a slim chance of survival if they could get "Aryan papers". My father's cousin, the one who had helped us get to Moscow, was soon reunited with his mother and his sister Elisabeth and her husband, Lutek. They had managed to get out of the Warsaw ghetto at the last minute, when only a few survivors remained. They were able to get papers and they stayed in an apartment until the Warsaw ghetto uprising in 1944. For all that time, Lutek, who looked unmistakably Jewish, hid in a tiny closet that had been fitted out for him.

Papa's other cousin, her husband and their two-year-old daughter had been killed. My cousin Inka, my playmate in Miedzeszyn, and her mother Sabina managed to survive. Waclaw, a friend of Sabina's who had been in love with her for years, saved them from certain death by getting them out of the ghetto and taking them away to a tiny village. He tried to save Inka's father too, but he died in the Warsaw uprising. Waclaw went back to the ghetto yet again to save Misha, Sabina's dog, who also survived the war!

Mama managed to find a few of her friends, those who had escaped from the ghetto with false papers. One of them had even survived concentration camp, along with her daughter. Another had been saved by a German officer who was smitten with her. Yet another had converted to Catholicism and had spent the war in her apartment, untroubled. She had a Polish lover, a married man who came to her apartment clandestinely. After the war, they were married.

So it was that we learned in bits and pieces who had survived and who — the vast majority — had died under the Nazi boot. We heard of heinous crimes, but also of acts of great heroism.

I listened to these stories, unable to breathe, and to this day they have stayed with me. I've never stopped thinking of those who died and those who survived, of the greatness and depravity of humans. And always I am haunted by the same question: what would I have done in their place? How would I have acted? I must admit that I have not yet found the answer.

Mikolaj, Uncle Yona's brother, was quite a wealthy man before the war. He had owned an umbrella factory in Riga, Lithuania. He was the one who had taken us in at Wilno and bought furniture for us. In the eyes of the Soviet regime, he was a bourgeois and therefore a criminal. That is why he was sent to a forced labour camp in Siberia. Towards the end of the war, he was liberated and assigned to live in a little town in Siberia. This was a common occurrence, and most of Siberia was populated by these former prisoners.

Mikolaj was quite an old man and his health was poor. He would have had no hope of surviving the terrible conditions and the harsh winters of Siberia, especially since all of his family who had remained in Riga had perished. He managed to get our address and sent us a letter of distress, and we tried to figure out how to bring him to Moscow. Mikolaj had been a Lithuanian national before the war but became a Soviet citizen after Lithuania was annexed to the Soviet Union in 1940. The Polish authorities in Moscow could do nothing for him. Some other way had to be found, and the solution my parents came up with was entirely illegal and extremely dangerous. They obtained the Polish passport of a deceased man, and my father decided to go fetch Mikolaj himself. In a country where a mere trifle could get you ten or twenty years in a concentration camp, such action could be punished by death. Still, my father would not give up the idea and began his preparations. He got a suitcase with a false bottom to hide the passport and a *laissez-passer*, bought a ticket for the voyage, and then he left.

Mama and I were sick with worry. However, everything went according to the careful plan. Mikolaj was waiting for Papa in the station restaurant. In the washroom, they took apart the false bottom of the suitcase and removed the documents needed to purchase Mikolaj's train ticket to Moscow. Mikolaj's genuine papers were torn up and flushed down the toilet, and Papa and Mikolaj returned to Moscow with no problem.

Mikolaj spent only one night with us. The following day, with another Polish passport in hand, he set off for Lvov, a transit point between the Soviet Union and Poland. This time, Mama accompanied him. As Mikolaj did not speak a word of Polish, he had to pretend to be a deaf-mute, while my mother did all the talking. Once again, all worked as planned, and Mama returned home safe and sound. We were greatly relieved and also immensely proud to have helped save one person's life.

Mikolaj did not stay in Poland long. He crossed the border into Germany illegally, and after all sorts of ups and downs, he settled in Palestine. Borders were easily crossed in the period right after the war, and many people took advantage of this fact to leave their country for good. The great majority of them were Jews who had survived the war in Poland or returned from Russia. The tragedy they had lived through had convinced them that they would be better off living somewhere else, especially when all their family and friends were gone. Mama said that "her" Warsaw no longer existed; it was nothing but a huge cemetery now.

So Mikolaj went to Palestine, which later became the

Jewish homeland, the state of Israel. He married again, made another fortune and lived for many long years. I think he knew of the great risks my parents had taken to get him out of Siberia, but he never really thanked them for what they had done. Many years later, I came across the memoirs he had written and given to his brother Yona. There was only one sentence about how he left Russia: "Michal came and got me out of there." I was a bit disappointed.

The Union of Polish Patriots was slowly disbanding. More and more of the exiles were returning to Poland. Our family managed to get a private room at the Severnaja, where we were still living. It was wonderful to have a bit more space and to be alone from time to time.

I wasn't much affected by all the departures, until the time came for Irena and her father to leave. This was a disaster for me. I had made no other friend but her among my classmates. I had no other real friends like my friends of Namangan.

Living conditions often made social life difficult. Most of the girls I knew lived in communal housing — large apartments that had belonged to wealthy families before the revolution. There was absolutely no privacy in these places and it was hard to do your homework in the common room, which was as crowded and busy as a railway station.

After Irena left, I spent a lot of time on my own, with books as my sole companions. I read a lot, mostly the classics of Russian literature. I learned whole poems by heart. I discovered the Polish writers Zeromski and Sienkiewicz, but I preferred Tolstoy and Turgenev. Although we spoke Polish at home, I had a much better and subtler command of Russian.

I was very lonely and I spent most of my time at home with my parents. Their marriage was on a rocky footing. My father had confessed that before the war he had had an affair with a woman who was now living in Moscow. He swore that the affair was definitely history. My mother believed him and, by coming to Moscow, showed how much she trusted him — out of love or naivety, who knows? Probably she was so afraid of the NKVD who had approached my father in Namangan that she didn't consider her personal feelings. My father gradually forgot his fine promises, and his old flame would not leave him alone, especially since there was no man in her life at the time. The atmosphere at home became hateful, with quarrels, tears and threats.

When Irena had still been there, I could escape and would often go out so that my parents could work out their problems. After she left, I couldn't help but get involved. Although I loved my father and didn't really understand affairs of the heart, I was one hundred percent on my mother's side. I couldn't understand why Mama didn't simply send him packing.

"Let's leave all this," I told her over and over. "The two of us will go to Poland."

But Mama could not imagine living without Papa. She loved him deeply, and he had never said outright that he wanted to leave her. I believe he was sincere. He would have been happy to live with two women in peace, but of course that was impossible.

Finally Mama decided that we would go back to Poland, and we began to get ready to leave. Papa said he would stay in Moscow a little while and join us later. We were not at all sure about this, since Papa's mistress didn't seem willing to give an inch.

Then, when everything was set for our departure, Mama swallowed a tube of sleeping pills. She was taken unconscious to the hospital and stayed there a few days. During this time, Papa continued to see his mistress, as if nothing had happened. I was furious with him and thought him unfeeling. But I understood Mama even less. How could she wish to kill herself over him? Why didn't she just leave him? And how could she fail to think of me? I was only sixteen, her only child whom she claimed to love above all else. This whole period was a very painful one.

Mama came home from the hospital and after long discussions with Papa, in which I wasn't included, they decided that all three of us would return together to Poland.

Our house in Miedzeszyn was occupied by people who had no intention of leaving, but there were two rooms waiting for us in a big apartment in Lodz, where Inka, Sabina and their "saviour" Waclaw were living. My feelings were confused. On the one hand I was happy to be back in the land of my earliest childhood, where all my family had lived, even though now only a few were left. On the other hand, I was a bit apprehensive. While we spoke Polish at home, I had had almost all of my schooling in Russian schools, and I was much more at ease in Russian. I had just finished Grade 9 and was reading the great Russian classics in the original, writing long compositions on them, and earning good marks. I wasn't sure I would do as well in a Polish school.

There were a few other worries as well. Rumours reached us from Poland that Jews were leaving, fearing the pogroms organized by Polish anti-Semites. This all seemed very frightening, and I imagined terrible scenes. My cousin Inka continued to live under her false identity from the occupation and was taking catechism classes at school!

On top of this was the Soviet propaganda railing against "reactionary forces" at work in Poland. It is true that many Poles felt a gut-wrenching hatred for the Soviet Union, which called itself the paradise of social justice. It is amazing that, even after witnessing so many horrible things, I still believed in that drivel. I was convinced that all the bad things arose from the war; once it was over, things would return to normal.

And yet a new wave of terror was already approaching. We heard that Russian soldiers returning from the war, in particular those who had survived the terrible Nazi camps, were being sent directly to Siberia, to equally terrible Soviet camps. The husband of a woman we knew had been shot as a spy upon his return from a German camp. But we spoke little of these things, for it was dangerous. And I, in my naivety and ignorance, thought that perhaps he really was a German spy.

And so I returned to Poland. I was sixteen years old, the war was over, a new life was about to begin. I was prey to certain fears but was also full of hopes and dreams, like any girl of that age.

Epilogue

Some things you remember your whole life long, while others are quickly forgotten. There are some blank spots in my memories, but certain vestiges of those years are so deeply rooted in my being that they will probably disappear only when I do. I would like to list them here, starting with the least important.

- When I see a piece of wood on the ground, I tell myself I should pick it up and use it to make a fire in our wood stove.

- Whenever I see a pile of horse's droppings, I think of what fine *kiziak* could be made from it.

- I'm always amazed that a one-kilogram loaf of bread can be so big.

- I always feel particularly drawn to pigs, especially piglets.

- I do not like dromedaries.

- I always try to keep a large supply of good-quality toilet paper at home.

- When my refrigerator at home seems empty and I'm about to go grocery shopping, I always think that a family of three could be fed for a good month on what I have left in the fridge.

- I always wanted to have several children. It seems to me that an only child has less chance of happiness in life.

- I have great faith in friendship and solidarity.

- A person who is hungry or has nowhere to sleep is always welcome in my home.

- I don't necessarily condemn thieves, for I know that sometimes theft is the only way to survive.

- I always give money to beggars.

- I am not afraid of having little money, because I know I can live on much less than what I possess.

- I firmly believe that courage and dignity will most often defeat physical strength.

- Whenever I move to a new apartment, I look for a spot that can be turned into a hiding place.

Montreal, November 1999

After the War

After the war Ilona and her family returned to Lodz in Poland, where she completed high school. She went on to lead a most remarkable life of achievement: first, she studied chemical engineering at the Department of Chemistry at the Polytechnical Institute of Warsaw, where she also studied for her Master's degree. She then worked in a pharmaceutical factory in Tarchomin, and after that, at the Pharmaceutical Institute. At the same time she earned a doctorate from the University of Warsaw. And all this she achieved while helping to run the household and raising her three children.

In 1968 the whole family immigrated to Canada. There Ilona was offered a position as Professor of Chemistry at the newly established French language University of Quebec, where she taught and supervised research for 23 years. Since her retirement she has undertaken the publication of memoirs of survivors of the Holocaust, under the auspices of the Polish Jewish Heritage Foundation. So far, she has helped the Foundation publish five books.

Over the years, Ilona told the stories of many of her experiences of the war years, first to her children and later to her grandchildren. When she retired, she wrote them down, first in Polish for her daughters, and then in

French for her grandchildren. Now, with this marvelous English translation, she is able to share with young adults everywhere this unique account of the things she saw, the experiences she lived through, and the hardships she overcame during her coming of age amidst the turmoil of the Second World War.